INTRODUCTION

The goal of THE UNIVERSAL TRAVELER is to provide a simplifying format for problem-solving. We believe that all problems, no matter what size they may be, can benefit from the same logical and orderly procedures now employed in the highly specialized, computer assisted statistical disciplines which address themselves to complex world problems. In principle our everyday and occasionally more important personal problems are no different than those larger issues. The process remains constant. It is only the methods which need to be changed, and then, often in appearance alone.

Since "Systems" is the general name assigned to Cybernetics and the various numerical techniques for modeling problem situations, we have similarly called our more conversational approach to problem-solving by the name "Soft-Systems." We intend the language and methods we have developed to help every reader deal more logically and systematically with the situations of their life. By becoming more conscious or aware of their own procedures and methods we ultimately expect to generate more creative problem-solvers at the world level.

Library of Congress Cataloging in Publication Data

Koberg, Don, 1930–
    The universal traveler.

    First experimental ed. published in 1973 under
title: The universal traveler: a companion for
those on problem-solving journeys and a soft-systems
guidebook to the process of design.
    1. Problem solving.   2.   Creation (Literary,
artistic, etc.)   I. Bagnall, Jim, joint author.
II. Title.
BF441.K55 1973   131'.32   73-15720
ISBN 0-913232-05-X

the ANATOMY of the Universal Traveler

INTRODUCTION
How the Universal Traveler
Can Help You------------------------4

the
EXPEDITION
OUTFITTER
P. 6

Introduction to CREATIVITY---------8
Keys to CREATIVE BEHAVIOR---------10
Blocks to CREATIVITY--------------14
THE DESIGN PROCESS----------------16
TRAVEL MAP------------------------18
A Word about METHODS--------------22
GENERAL TRAVEL TIPS---------------23
GENERAL LANGUAGE GUIDE------------26
GENERAL TRAVEL GUIDE--------------27
BACK HOME WITH MEMORABILIA------101

THE
UNIVERSAL
TRAVEL
AGENCY
P. 29

Why Use a Travel Agency--30
Checklists---------------31
Tourist Traps------------31
The Birth
   of a Problem-----------34
ACCEPTANCE----------------36
ANALYSIS------------------46
DEFINITION----------------59
IDEATION------------------66
IDEA-SELECTING------------74
IMPLEMENTATION------------80
EVALUATION----------------94

a. Introduction
b. Language Guide
c. Methods
d. Travel Guides
e. Travel Tips

SIDE
TRIPS
P. 103

Creativity Games------------------104
Guide to Measurable Objectives--108
Lessons from Problem-Solving----110
Synectics-------------------------114
Self-Hypnotism--------------------116
Painless Criticism---------------118
Communications Checklist--------118
Wiring Diagrams-------------------121

INDEX

38136

How the Universal Traveler can help YOU

Although we expect it to be self-evident, here is the way in which THE UNIVERSAL TRAVEL has been designed to work for you:
Throughout you will find continual references to the process of design as a journey or excursion. This symbolic "travel-ese" is used in order to reinforce the concept that design is more meaningful when it can be visualized and pursued as a logical, planned journey through a series of ENERGY STATES and not simply taken as a random, chance process.

Before beginning any serious journey, it is well to stop at THE EXPEDITION OUTFITTER, where general advice and information is available for the kinds of tools and equipment you may require for the trip. The "OUTFITTER" can also provide TRAVEL TIPS or hints, LANGUAGE GUIDES or notes on the semantics of foreign tongues, and GUIDEBOOKS and additional references, including a TRAVEL MAP.

The central part of the book is named THE UNIVERSAL TRAVEL AGENCY because it is the information storehouse for journeys of all kinds. In it you will find the methods for getting started and for proceeding along toward the various points on your itinerary. Much in the same way that we select different ways to travel to different destinations in life, we also need to tailor our design journeys by selecting appropriate methods for each of those unique trips. The UNIVERSAL TRAVEL AGENCY contains many alternative vehicles for traveling and it emphasizes the movement or transition from one ENERGY STATE to another

within the total sequence of steps in the
design process. THE UNIVERSAL TRAVEL
AGENCY section is sub-divided into the seven
major phases or ENERGY STATES so that the
traveler might take a sample problem through
the process in an efficient manner.

Additional TRAVEL TIPS, LANGUAGE GUIDES and
GUIDEBOOKS are provided within each of these
seven sections.

The final part of THE UNIVERSAL TRAVELER is
called SIDE TRIPS. It contains some information which can enhance or enrich each journey
and make it more meaningful. SIDE TRIPS are
like bonuses for extra effort in problem-
solving.

All travel guides are forever in need of
updating, so THE UNIVERSAL TRAVELER has been
printed with a wide margin on each page to
provide plenty of room for your notes. As
you discover methods of your own and adapt
them to better meet your personal needs, it
would be helpful to you to write them down on
these pages. Then, you won't have to rediscover
them every time you embark on a new journey.
As for other things the value of books derives
from the benefit they provide to you. When
you fill-in the margins and borders you will
also be personalizing this copy and thereby
deriving a greater value for your participation.

BON VOYAGE

Get everything you need to take along at

the
EXPEDITION
OUTFITTER

✓ hiking boots
rain slicker
fur-lined gloves
✓ safety matches
flashlight
✓ batteries

There is nothing more important to the comfort
of any journey than the tools, food and equipment we need along the way. When our gear is
insufficient or mis-matched to the circumstances,
everything else seems to lose its importance.
BE PREPARED. In THE EXPEDITION OUTFITTER you
find a summary discussion of CREATIVITY and
its destructive counterpart FEAR.

A descriptive map of the general route into
and through a problem is also provided. Then
a brief note about DESIGN METHODS - selecting
alternate means and the custom-planned itinerary
is followed by several pages of general TRAVEL
 TIPS. NOTE CAREFULLY! Many cautious travelers
have been saved from disaster by heeding such
tips and forewarnings.

A library of TRAVEL GUIDES fills the final
section of THE OUTFITTER. Here are guides to
the strange languages and manners of speaking
you may find when away from home. Some of
these guides are travelogs about specific
trips previous travelers have made and others
contain advice of a general nature.

After reading THE OUTFITTER you may also find
it helpful to breeze through the remainder
of the book to the SIDE TRIPS section at the
end. There, the GUIDE TO MEASURABLE OBJECTIVES
may be found and put to immediate use for
saving time and energy at the outset of your
trip.

After looking the entire book over, you will
be in a better position to custom-tailor the
alternative routes and methods outlined in
the main body of the text. Take it slowly
and easily the first couple of times through
the process. Travel is a lot more fun when
you are not always on the run.

INTRODUCTION to CREATIVITY

The DESIGN PROCESS is a sequence of events which demands creative behavior from its participants. Its activity is to improve existing conditions and to find clear paths out of dilemmas.

In order to improve existing conditions, it is necessary to become aware first of the problematic state (the general situation or thing that needs improving); second of the essential components of the problem and, third of the skills and methods required to manipulate that problem condition into a better state.

Creativity can be defined as both the art and the science of thinking and behaving with both subjectivity and objectivity. It is a combination of feeling and knowing; of alter-nating back and forth between what we sense and what we already know. Becoming more creative involves becoming awake to both; dis-covering a state of wholeness which differs from the primarily objective or subjective person which typifies our society. For example: The primarily OBJECTIVE person, be-ing a knower after the fact, briefly senses the surrounding natural and man-made environ-ment and then determines the existence of logic and beauty within that experience. The primarily SUBJECTIVE person, being a here-and-now sense mechanism, proceeds as a continuum of sensory response, delighting in sensory experience, caring little for fixed conclusions. TO COMBINE THE TWO IS TO GAIN MORE THAN BOTH: A more natural and conscious balance between extremes. Such 'creative' wholeness allows us to see ourselves from above...to both lead our way and to follow that way...to both deter-mine our goal and to go: to both design the stimulus and to experience the response.

Although sometimes necessary, problem solu-tions which merely 'work' and do no more do not represent what we can refer to as 'creative solutions'. CREATIVE PROBLEM SOLUTIONS are different...they are those

8

which lead, which inspire, which provoke;
those which help us to imagine more advanced
problems or which provide us with the models
for solving other, similar problems. They
turn us on to their correctness and obvious-
ness or simplicity. Creative Problem-Solvers
therefore are persons who intend to go beyond
mere function and stability; who have occupa-
tional needs for developing certain behavioral
attributes for creativity or conscious
difference.

It is simple enough to list those "attributes
of creative difference" and to point out the
reasons for their importance. But actual
development and refinement of such behavioral
characteristics is difficult since society
makes it a relentless battle, an often
thankless and rarely positively reinforced
chore to maintain such behavior.

The typically "abnormal" behavior of the
creative person may be described by normal
society as boorish, prideless, maladjusted,
careless, even unpatriotic and a menace to
the 'institutions' which the average person
builds to perpetuate 'average' or 'normal'
behavior.

The same society which readily accepts the
creative 'product' will chastise or deny the
creative 'activity' required for such production because of its non-typical nature.

Schools, operated by the perpetuation of
"average" and administration-oriented persons,
punish all hints of 'wholeness' behavior. And
although we say that we expect our schools to
engender creativity, we usually also allow a
continuation of the discipline-over-development
approach to discouraging creative growth in
our young. When the human product emerges
as a non-creative, average sample, we do not
complain; instead we alter the meaning of
creativity to describe other abnormal human
activities such as condoning high productivity
as a creative act. So, in a very special
sense, the creative person is abnormal:
different from the others and therefore often
subject to their disapproval and discourage-
ment.

DESIGNERS TAKE NOTE!! If your human
relations are on a smooth course, it is
probable that one of two alternatives is
in effect: either you are not being creative
or you have conditioned yourself and the
others in your environment to accept your
abnormal behavior.

9

Some keys to Creative Behavior

People become more and more creative by simply becoming more conscious of what it is they do and of how what they do relates to what is in their environment. Said another way, creativity and consciousness of procedures (process) and methods go hand in hand. If you become more aware of your position relative to what has gone before and what is yet to come, your ability to decide from both the broad view and the specific view is increased. If you become more conscious of the stages of the process you can become more accurate in your predictions for what to do next. And you can become more skilled at choosing better ways to move forward as you become more conscious of what work such methods must perform.

Along with developing a consciousness of process and methods, here are a few more keys to creativity:

1. Freedom from False Pride
2. Belief in One's Own Ability to Succeed
3. Constructive Discontent
4. Wholeness
5. Ability to Control Habit

Keys 1

SELF-DISCIPLINE OR FREEDOM FROM FALSE PRIDE

Self-discipline, or as Bobby Seale defines it, "behaving the same," is another way to say "freedom from false pride." (Pride is used here as a general term for the hangups associated with a lack of <u>self-discipline</u>). To be able to "hold your head up high" with pride is destructive counter-creative behavior. It is difficult to see well from that position and detracts from the positive attainment of goals. False pride stands in the way of creativity by inhibiting us from asking key questions, thus stifling the key requisite for curiosity. It restricts a change of mind or direction which thereby fixes a pre-conceived and prejudicial course. And it runs counter to the true selflessness required for the 'giving' of oneself to the task! False pride sets up a potential for being untrue to one's self. It joins the other six "deadly sins" - greed, lust, sloth, envy, gluttony and hate - and diverts our attention from improvement.

Contrary to false pride, Self-Discipline is a truth-reality behavior. "Behaving the same" requires the courage of convictions and the freedom from fear of social reprisal. It is a fearless acceptance of the responsibility of being what we are, knowing what we know and do not know and of taking the steps required to insure our own development. Self-discipline encourages an ever-enlarging knowledge, an increased sensitivity and the formation of a true philosophy of freedom...not the false freedom of pride through autonomy, belonging or ownership. Through self-discipline, we constantly strengthen our own positions; through pride we weaken them.

Self-discipline does not mean 'doing your thing' contrary to the needs of the group, and it does not mean that we cannot tailor our approach to the specific situations within which we find ourselves. But it does limit unreal behavior, untrue or devious behavior, 'kind lies' and self-righteous behavior. It does not restrict us from performing tasks which we believe to be necessary although unpleasant. But it does eliminate the waste-ful acting out of many irrelevant social demands.

BELIEF IN ONE'S ABILITY TO SUCCEED

Ego-strength is not an ego-trip. A belief in one's own ability is not a license to become a blowhard: It is simply a necessary trait for the further development of creative behavior. Encourage yourself. Get yourself moving (motivated). If you wait for someone else to move you, it is possible to find yourself headed in an uncomfortable direction.

Contrary to developing this necessary trait, we often spend much of our time playing the social game of self-denial; of publicly denying our abilities and potentials; of enjoying the 'popularity' of being 'humble' and of generally declaring that we don't think we'll make it. It is simply not socially acceptable to construct ego-strength or unique personal be-liefs while being very acceptable to express

11

total vulnerability to the group. Because
of such pressures, we are often forced to
express self-belief in private. The result
is that self-esteem must be 'dragged out of
us'; the more deeply we bury it, the more
remote it becomes from being part of our
behavior pattern. "Begin to believe in
your own creative potential and you will
begin to be more creative" is a requisite
attitude to creative growth.

CONSTRUCTIVE DISCONTENT

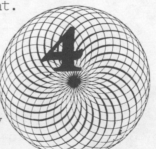

Arrival at adolescence is usually all that
is required for achieving half of this
important attribute of creativity. It is
unusual to find a 'contented' young person;
discontent goes with that time of life. To
the young, everything needs improvement.
Yet, it is usually the lack of a constructive
attitude which wins out in the end, turning
all of that healthy 'discontent' into nothing
more than a "bunch of gripes."

As we age, our discontent wanes; we learn
from our society that 'fault-finders' disturb
the status quo of the normal, average
'others.' Squelch tactics are introduced.
It becomes 'good' not to 'make waves' or
'rock the boat' and to 'let sleeping dogs
lie' and 'be seen but not heard.' It is
'good' to be invisible and enjoy your
'autonomy.' It is 'bad' to be a problem-
maker. And so everything is upside-down for
creativity and its development. Thus,
constructive attitudes are necessary for a
dynamic condition; discontent is prerequisite
to problem-solving. Combined, they define a
primary quality of the creative problem-solver:
a constantly developing Constructive Discontent.

WHOLENESS

Everyone both senses and knows. It is
natural to both feel and decide. Yet, it is
also normal to tend to smother our sensitivity
in favor of strengthening our expression of
judgment. Society says that it's better to
know than it is to feel. It just seems more
'grown-up' that way because that's the way
most people are. BUT WAIT A MINUTE. We know
that creative people are different from 'most
people.' It just might be more creative of us
if we didn't stifle our emotions, but instead
allowed those 'feelings' to enter into the
conscious world of our knowing responses.
Perhaps we could continue to both sense and
respond with knowledge. This need not mean
that we have to become super-sensitive and

forget all about knowing. It simply means that we could attempt to redesign our behavior into a more balanced whole; to alternate between feeling and knowing; between sensing and deciding in a conscious way. And thus be more in control of our whole potential.

5

ABILITY TO CONTROL HABIT

The things that keep most of us from behaving creatively are our habits. A habit is behavior which is preconceived; when you have a habit, you already know how to do something. Of course, there are good habits and bad habits and the value judgment is determined by how helpful or hindering your habits become to your problem-solving ability. For instance, all of our intuition (sub-conscious response) is previously learned behavior (or habit) which works at times for us and at other times against us. From the beginning of life we learn, and we commit that learning to our memory. Afterwards we tend to behave in ways which reflect our learning. It's perfectly O.K. to be intuitive; in fact it would be impossible not to be...almost all of what we do is intuitive and we learn most of that before we reach eight years. But it is very important to the creative process that we don't allow ourselves to get locked into our intuition and its preconceived approach to life. To be able to see things in different ways and to remain innovative it is absolutely necessary to be in control of our habits... always ready to take a chance on the unproven and to discard them when they get in the way of a clear view.

 Steady creativity requires a steady, determined effort. The more consistently we behave in ways which encourage creativity, the more likely we are to be consistently creative. Creativity is a learnable state of behavior patterns. It is not magic. And it is not a quirk of birth. Some people don't "just have it." Creativity demands listening to your own logical and sensitive conclusions, not only to the dictates of the immediate environment or society. In a mass society, conformity is the shortest route to acceptance by our peers. To become unique is a sure way to become an outcast...or at least not always

accepted. But true difference comes automatically to the creative...who by intention
are prideless, adventurous, self-disciplined
and self-believing...who have an interest in
resolving problematic conditions in a positive
way and...who are learning to develop their
ability to be 'whole.' These are the keys
to creativity. To make them work for us to
unlock the reality of a 'whole' participation
in our world we must first discover them to be
true for ourselves through personal experience
and to then adapt them to our everyday behavior.

Blocks to creativity

There are many opportunities to be wrong. But
few of them carry stiff penalties. Still out
of fear of being wrong most of us seem to be
waiting until we know it all; until we are the
world "experts" before we can speak up or act
up to a situation. Yet few of us ever seem to
become that world "expert." Therefore, we are
kept from creativity by our own pride, fear,
jealousy and competitiveness. We block our
own creativity by:

    FEAR OF making mistakes
    FEAR OF being seen as a fool
    FEAR OF being criticized
    FEAR OF being misused
    FEAR OF being "alone" (a
        person with an idea is
        automatically a
        minority of one)
    FEAR OF disturbing traditions
        and making changes
    FEAR OF being associated
        with taboos
    FEAR OF losing the security
        of habit
    FEAR OF losing the love of
        the group
    FEAR OF truly being an individual

Being afraid is both natural and normal.
It would be a mistake to think we could
eliminate it altogether, nor would we
want to. Fear is simply the reluctance
and anxiety to deal with the unexpected or
the result of lack of preparation to deal with
the expected. But fear deters progress toward
creativity through misdirecting our energy
and by restraining us from the action necessary
to its development. By changing our focus
from "I don't want to be wrong" to "I will
try to be right" the positive point of view
can overcome this general block to creativity.

14

Logic is...

In essence logic helps us to understand how
all things are or can be organized and interrelated. Logic provides the ground rules of
all organization. Logic helps sensory response (or "sense") find meaning. In short

logic makes sense.

(Organized knowing develops meaningful feeling)

LOGIS IS a basis
LOGIC IS a guide for mental
   activity
LOGIC IS devoid of every-
   day linguistic content
   It has no semantics
LOGIC IS syntax rather than
   definition
LOGIC IS structure
LOGIC IS a priori--not a
   posteriori
LOGIC IS a series of
   operations or method-
   ical transformations
LOGIC IS axiomatic if it
   is two-valued (right
   or wrong) (either/or)
LOGIC IS probabilistic if
   it is multi-valued
   (conditional) (both/
   and)
LOGIC IS not metaphysical.
   It is very real
LOGIC IS the basic scientific
   method
LOGIC IS a mental exercise
   when considered by
   itself
LOGIC IS simply organiza-
   tional. It is a new
   thing when meaning is
   incorporated
   viz; architecture,
   physics, psychology, etc.
LOGIC IS in flux. It grows
   with scientific discovery

15

The DESIGN PROCESS is a Problem-Solving JOURNEY

Since all of us, more or less, embark on many problem-solving journeys, each of us is, more or less, involved in the design process. The more we understand about DESIGN PROCESS, the more interesting and meaningful will be our problem-solving journeys.

Design can be defined as the process of creative problem-solving; a process of creative, constructive behavior. Designers are people who behave creatively relative to problem situations; people who generate uniquely satisfying solutions to such situations. Gym teachers and geology majors, free-lance writers and truck farmers, movie makers and motorcyclists, audiophiles and elevator operators, xylophonists and ZOOM fans are all problem-solvers. Everyone is a problem-solver. Some just do it better than others.

The PROCESS of DESIGN or creative problem-solving describes a series or sequence of events, stages, phases or ENERGY STATES, as we will call them. Before completing a total design journey, it is usually necessary to pass through each of those phases. Once each phase is known through experience, the design process as a whole can be appreciated as a round-trip which includes intentions, decisions, solutions, actions and evaluations. There are seven such ENERGY STATES given. Each has been chosen as a synthesis from many models of process.*

*Wallas, Dewey, Rossman, Guilford, Osborn, Stanislawski, Parnes, Gordon, Kepner-Tregoe, Arnold, Churchman, Zwicky, General Electric, the Military, Pert, etc.

The logical sequence of events included in the design process is:

accept situation

TO FIND REASONS FOR GOING ON:
To state initial intentions.
To accept the problem as
a challenge; to give up
our autonomy to the prob-
lem and allow the problem
to become our process.

analyse

TO GET THE FACTS AND FEELINGS:
To get to know about the
ins and outs of the problem;
to discover what the world
of the problem looks like.

define

TO DETERMINE THE ESSENTIAL GOAL(S):
To decide what we believe
to be the main issues of
the problem; to conceptu-
alize and to clarify our
major goals concerning
the problem situation.

ideate

TO GENERATE OPTIONS FOR
ACHIEVING THE ESSENTIAL GOAL(S):
To search out all the ways
of possibly getting to the
major goals. Alternatives.

select

TO CHOOSE FROM THE OPTIONS:
To compare our goals as defined
with our possible ways of getting
there. Determine best ways to go.

implement

TO TAKE ACTION (OR PLAN TO ACT):
To give action or physical
form to our selected "best
ways."

evaluate

TO REVIEW AND PLAN AGAIN:
To determine the effects or
ramifications as well as the
degree of progress of our design
activity.

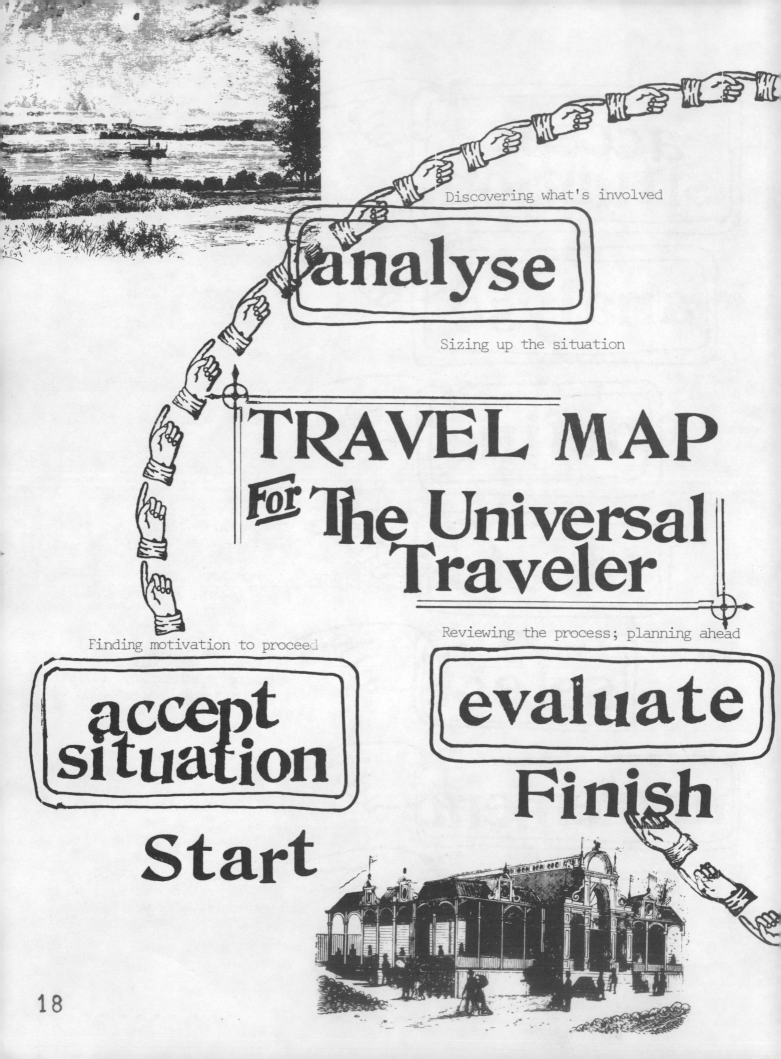

Discovering what's involved

analyse

Sizing up the situation

TRAVEL MAP
For The Universal Traveler

Reviewing the process; planning ahead

Finding motivation to proceed

accept situation

evaluate
Finish

Start

Developing conceptual guidelines

define

Generating optional ways for satisfying your definitions

ideate

The Creative Process of Problem-Solving or Design is like taking an excursion or JOURNEY!

select

Choosing; deciding between the options

Taking action on your decision

implement

19

The basic function of using a conscious format for increased creativity within the problem-solving activity of design is to free us from uncertainty, anxiety, confusion and other in-securities as we travel along our journey. It is an organizational guide which can help us to better enjoy the trip by allowing us to concentrate more on our creative participation rather than on whether or not we are moving toward or away from planned destinations.

Knowledge and use of the DESIGN PROCESS provides a fuller, richer and productive life by allowing us to take conscious control of our own life process--as opposed to being the passive victim of the decisions of others and/or the consequences of nature.

The design process can be viewed in a variety of ways. Some see it as a <u>linear</u> thing; others see it as a circular configuration.

linear

Where one thing follows another in a straight line.

accept situation ➡ analyse ➡ define ➡ ideate ➡ select ➡ implement ➡ evaluate

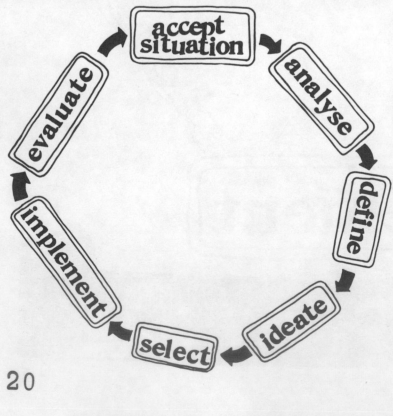

circular

Where there is continuity, but never a beginning and end. As one problem situation appears to be resolved, another one appears to begin.

20

feedback

Others see it as a constant feedback system where you never go forward without always looping back to check on yourself; where one progresses by constant backward relationships and where the stages of the process advance somewhat concurrently until some strong determining variable terminates the process (time, money, energy, etc.)

accept situation → analyse → define → ideate → select → implement → evaluate

branching

And still others see the design process as a branching system where certain events determine more than one direction and where directional progress is achieved via a many-branched excursion.

accept situation → analyse → ideate / define → select → implement → evaluate / re-analyse

accept situation → define → ideate / re-analyse → ideate → select

As a matter of fact and practicality, it really doesn't make too much difference how you view it. The design process is a round-trip of phases which begins at one point and goes outward from there and back again. If the excursion has been logically pursued, a systematic trek through all of the energy states has been made. If the trip has been meaningful, the return to the place of beginning shows it to be a different place than when you left. The journey has become, because of your new experiences, a new and exciting thing. From this point of view, the design process can be seen as not merely circular or helical, but rather as a SPIRAL CONTINUUM of sequential round trips which becomes a basic model, perhaps, like the DNA molecule, for all existence.

a word about Problem-Solving Methods

By now you should be able to view the process of creative problem-solving (Design Process) as a varied multi-stage experience. It includes an excursion through seven (7) different phases or energy states. Since travel within those phases is sometimes simple and yet at times complex, the well-seasoned problem solver usually carries a varied bag of techniques or approaches to help along the way. Design Methods is the common name given to such techniques for advancing into and through the phases of the process. They are merely practical ways for getting from one energy state to another.

There are as many different methods as there are people with needs for methods. Designing methods of your own is easy once you realize they need not be complex or formal. Our favorite methods are called "Take a chance" and "Write it down." A general rule for choosing methods is to find and use those which best fit both the problem and the problem solver. To follow that rule and to tailor the methods to both problem and problem solver is a separate task within each problem-solving journey. It is a task similar to that of selecting the route, side roads and overnight stops for an auto trip. Just as any competent trip planner would examine the alternate routes on a map and read through several brochures, books or articles before choosing a route for a trip, so should the problem solver read through the methods which follow, attempt to comprehend their simple techniques and be unafraid to adapt any of them to special or personal needs or to write additional ones to meet individualized problem requirements. Common sense suggests that complex problems may utilize complex techniques while simple problems might be handled by simpler tools. It should be clear, in any event, that just as you wouldn't choose a moving van to go get the groceries, you would not attempt to use computerized techniques in order to determine your choice of entrees on a menu.

the BEST technique is the ONE which works BEST for YOU!

General Travel Tips

BEFORE BEGINNING YOUR PROBLEM-SOLVING JOURNEY you may want to check the following "tips" that have been passed down from seasoned travelers.

Design is a process of making your dreams come true. Once you decide what you desire to be improved, it's almost certain that you will find many ways to make it happen.

An old Zen motto: 'If you want to get someplace, you've got to give up wanting to get to that place'; 'In order to achieve something, you've got to stop waiting for it to happen and get into the process of achieving it.' Life is a <u>process</u> which has many spin-offs called <u>products</u>.

NOTE! Keep a sharp lookout for the face of the well-seasoned traveler on the left above. His tips on conditions ahead are invaluable.

The creative person needs to be assertive and often a maker of problems. If too much autonomy and privacy is sought the experience of seeing new problem situations may be reduced.

Although design involves making our own dreams come true, the designer should take care not to become an 'impossible dreamer.'

When you arrive at the end of a journey, you are merely ready to begin the next one. Life is a helix. Commencement means both to start and to finish.

It is important not to view the phases of the design process as fixed things or points in time. It is better to think of them as whole states through which we pass and within which we spend different amounts of time. Such a view improves our understanding of process as a universal life concept.

Don't fall in love with an idea. There are so many of them; they are truly expendable. It is only after an idea is translated into reality that it becomes valuable.

To help recognize problems, we must begin to view them as 'situations in need of improvement.'

"Talking about it" needs to be balanced by "trying it out." Theory and practice must combine for wholeness.

Attitudes change with practical experience (learn by doing).

If you want to learn about something, try teaching it to someone else. No one ever learns as much as the teacher.

Inventions are easy. It's the job of making them work and getting them into use which is so hard.

There are billions of problems which could occupy your energy; deciding the ones which are right for you takes careful selection. It's a good idea to realize that you don't have time to solve them all.

Relax occasionally during the problem-solving process. Some people call this allowing enough time to 'incubate'; allowing your thoughts to become behavior. We all need time to 'digest' what we eat, before chewing some more.

Avoid the trap of prejudice. Prejudice means pre-judging; knowing the answer before you begin. Try to remember to Defer Judgment until all the facts are known.

Process orientation is a living involvement. It is usually more highly productive than an orientation toward production.

Try not to get so locked into a habit that it will cost you heavily to break. Habit-breaking is a necessity of creative problem-solving.

The more methods you have time to use or have the facility to use, the better off you will be in the long run. If you could travel by foot, auto, bus and plane, the combined view would be broader than by any one means.

Don't select a method which doesn't feel good. But try to realize that you often have to test new things in order to break them in.

Listen to your problems. Talk to them and about them. Write about them. Feel their "temperature." When all your senses are in tune with the problem, you should have a common sense view.

The anxiety of not knowing if you can succeed will be easily replaced by a simple time-task schedule.

Caution: Using the same method over and over again may become hazardous to your problem-solving health. Try several methods for each phase of the problem-solving journey.

Rather than saving evaluation until after the trip is completed, a simpler way is to make incremental notes as you go.

Make analogy-finding one of your pass-times. Pick some random thing around you and find ten things that are like it in some way. Finding interrelationships is a most creative activity.

Subjective emotions naturally precede objective knowledge. We only know what we feel to be true from experience. The rest is conjecture or faith.

To make a good decision, it often becomes necessary to project ourselves into the future to "see" whether or not our idea will make sense tomorrow.

The statute of limitations on problem-solutions is short. Because problems are never solved for very long, the profession with the brightest future is that of creative problem-solving.

The process-oriented problem solver who keeps a good record (words, pictures, plans, souvenirs, etc.) will have a far greater product than the product-oriented problem solver without a record of the rush to meet a goal.

Dealing with general problems requires knowledge of generalized principles. As Bucky Fuller says...we should "get a really grand strategy for dealing with the whole."

For each different situation we must quickly determine what we can count on and what we can't. Dependent and independent variables must be identified and grouped.

General Language Guide

THE DESIGN PROCESS

A PROCESS OF maximizing goals
A PROCESS OF optimizing objectives
A PROCESS OF realizing intentions
A PROCESS OF giving form to intentions
A PROCESS OF making dreams come true
A PROCESS OF anticipatory improvement
A PROCESS OF bridging analysis to
　　　　　　synthesis via concept
A PROCESS OF taking apart, comprehending
　　　　　　and putting together
A PROCESS OF organizing data into improved
　　　　　　reality
A PROCESS OF fulfilling a prophecy

DESIGN METHODS

TECHNIQUES
TOOLS FOR PROBLEM-SOLVING
STRATEGIES
WAYS FOR DOING THINGS
DIRECTIONS FOR ADVANCEMENT THROUGH A
　PROBLEM-SOLVING PROCESS
TRICKS

PHASES OF THE DESIGN PROCESS

ACTIVITIES OF CREATIVE PROBLEM-SOLVING
STEPS TOWARD A GOAL
ANALYSIS-SYNTHESIS
SEQUENCE OF PROBLEM-SOLVING EVENTS
CHECKPOINTS TOWARD SOLUTION-FINDING
LEVELS OF INVOLVEMENT
ENERGY STATES
STAGES OF PROBLEM-SOLVING ACCOMPLISHMENT

THE CREATIVE PERSON

a dealer in options
a logical problem-solver
a habit-breaker
a constructively discontented person
a divergent-convergent thinker
innovative
a fearless adventurer
a whole person
a person who enjoys being off center
unpredictable
a lovable jerk
behaves differently from others

General Travel Guides

Adams, J., Portable Stanford
CONCEPTUAL BLOCKBUSTING

Alexander, C., Harvard University Press
NOTES ON THE SYNTHESIS OF FORM

Bruner, J., Atheneum
ON KNOWING

Carpenter, E., Ballantine
THEY BECAME WHAT THEY BEHELD

Churchman, C.W., Basic Books
THE DESIGN OF AN INQUIRING SYSTEM

DeBono, E., Basic Books
THE FIVE-DAY COURSE IN THINKING

DeBono, E., Basic Books
NEW THINK; The Use of Lateral Thinking

Fabun, D., Editor, Kaiser Alum. News
ON CREATIVITY

Fuller, R. B., Doubleday
INTUITION

Gaskin, Stephen, Book Farm
MONDAY NIGHT CLASS

Gardner, J. W., Harper and Row
SELF-RENEWAL

Gordon, Wm., Collier
SYNECTICS

Gordon, Wm., Porpoise
THE METAPHORICAL WAY

Harrisberger, L., Brooks/Cole
ENGINEERSMANSHIP

Interaction ASSOC. Inc., San Francisco
STRATEGY NOTEBOOK

Jones, J. C., Wiley
DESIGN METHODS

Koberg, D. and Bagnall, J., Wm. Kaufmann
VALUES TECH

Mager, R., Fearon
GOAL ANALYSIS

Mager, R., Fearon
PREPARING INSTRUCTIONAL OBJECTIVES

Maltz, M., Wilshire
PSYCHO-CYBERNETICS

_____, State Univ. of N.Y. (Buffalo)
JOURNAL OF CREATIVE BEHAVIOR
   INSTITUTE OF CREATIVE BEHAVIOR

MacKinnon, D. W., Am. Psych. 1962
XVII, 484-495
THE NATURE AND NURTURE OF CREATIVE TALENT

McPherson, J. H., Pendell
THE PEOPLE THE PROBLEMS AND THE
   PROBLEM SOLVING METHODS

Osborn, A., Scribners
APPLIED IMAGINATION

Parnes/Harding, Scribners
THE SOURCE BOOK FOR CREATIVE THINKING

Parnes, S., Scribners
THE CREATIVE BEHAVIOR GUIDEBOOK

Parnes, S., Scribners
THE CREATIVE BEHAVIOR WORKBOOK

Polya, G., Doubleday
HOW TO SOLVE IT

Sanoff, H., N.C. State
TECHNIQUES OF EVALUATION FOR DESIGNERS

Simon, H. A., Basic Books
THE SCIENCES OF THE ARTIFICIAL

Stein, M. I., Academic Press
STIMULATING CREATIVITY

Whiting, G., Reinhold
CREATIVE THINKING

Potter, J. H., Van Nostrand
HANDBOOK OF THE ENGINEERING SCIENCES
   VOLS. I & II

Zwicky, F., et al, Springer-Verlag (N.Y.)
NEW METHODS OF THOUGHT AND PROCEDURE

·the·
··· UNIVERSAL ···
TRAVEL AGENCY

A storehouse of means & methods for getting from
HERE THERE

Why Use a Travel Agency?

The Universal Travel Agency is the place to go when planning a problem-solving trip. There you may discover many of the various methods for wending your way through the problem-solving process in a more creative way.

Each of the seven sections within the "Agency" represents the progressive stages (or Energy States) of the logical problem-solving sequence. Within each of those segments you will find an Introduction to that part, a series of possible Methods or techniques for you to sample as aids to passing successfully through that state, some specific Travel Tips regarding the environment of that state, a Language Guide and a brief list of helpful references or Travel Guide.

Although it is theoretically efficient and therefore generally ideal to progress through each state in sequence, it is also normal to vary the sequence in accord with the specific demands of each problem and problem solver. In the end, the most logical procedure is that special series of events which works best for you and your problem.

Remember: Design Methods are merely means or techniques which facilitate certain activities. You will probably discover and adapt those methods which best meet your own needs quite naturally as well as attempting to invent your own. By getting to know how to use a large number of methods, you increase your skill and potential as a creative problem solver just as increasing your vocabulary would increase your ability to speak with greater clarity and insight.

Checklists

Everyone would like to find a universally useful design method. Checklist-making comes close to filling that wish. Throughout the design process it is useful to make lists of questions and answers for anything and everything related to each of the seven Energy States. Such lists form an outline of the entire problem situation and are important entries in any record of the process. Checklists are not only useful for records, but also provide guidance for further action; things to do; places to visit; people to see; etc. By accepting the task of making a series of checklists, you provide yourself a means to review the entire problem (similar to another popular method known as Program Evaluation Review Technique or PERT). They are a handy way to jot down ideas as they come along for possible use at a later date. When your lists increase in size and number, they can be reorganized and combined to simplify dealing with the problem as a whole and to clarify its parts.

Checklists are really no different from grocery lists. They help you organize your task and provide an overall view of the situation, its requirements, attributes, alternatives and consequences.

Tourist Traps

Some things to approach with caution on your problem-solving journey...

☞1 Don't be afraid of your intuition. It is your background knowledge; your basic reference data-bank. Intuition is what we call our inside knowledge based on past experience. It governs our reaction to new situations based on what we perceive it to be from the viewpoint of our old experiences. It is our past coming forward as a judge of our future.

Trust and respect your intuition...but don't allow it to control all your decisions. Try to use both new analysis as well as old experience to judge both new and old situations.

Try not to get caught in the typical tourist predicament of arriving home after an exciting journey without clear records of your experience (written in terms of what your objectives had been from the start).

Novice tourists return with two bags of dirty laundry, a few half-empty matchbook covers, a travel brochure for a side trip never taken, unwritten postcards, several slides of the "Eiffel Tower in the fog" and an intense desire to go back again next year to "do it right."

The well-seasoned traveler on the other hand keeps an itinerary and record book at all times for collecting names and addresses, making sketches, gluing in supplements, photos, ticket stubs, programs, etc. Return trips are more valuable and pleasurable as evaluating past records leads to new ventures.

Problem-solving travelers need to rely on both physical and mental health in order to function completely and properly. It's a cinch that when we don't feel well, whether consciously or subconsciously, we can't be able to operate at full potential.

Warning: Don't let your nerves get shattered by drinking too much coffee or tea.

Don't eat too much non-nutritive, fatty, low energy foods (eat a high protein peanut butter sandwich instead of a candy bar).

Don't expect to operate well without sleep. When tired, take a nap and then proceed on your journey.

BEWARE of falling into the trap of over-valuing your initial progress. There is usually much more traveling to do.

A "first" idea can end up being your "only" idea and get you into lots of trouble if it is not properly evaluated in terms of your objectives.

Consciousness of what you do allows you to consider alternatives and to make constant comparisons with your intentions or goals.

Don't be frightened by the bigness or smallness of things. There are tools for dealing with almost all contexts. Look for the tools that fit the task.

Ideas only have true meaning when they can become the logical fulfillment of design objectives.

Experience is the best teacher. You can only know what you discover for yourself to be true.

 **6** The older, more educated and experienced you become, the more you know and the less sense you imagine to need. That is, as you age and get smarter you tend to give up the need for sensitivity and to replace it with the knowledge gained through using your senses in the past. You become a know-it-all and a sense-it-not.

Remember that wholeness requires both sensitivity and knowledge. It helps to enhance curiosity, uniqueness, doing the unexpected and adventure.

 **7** When problem situations arise
Don't do the natural thing and ask
"What can I do about it?"

That question will only give you ideas or ways to solve a situation which has not yet been defined. It will give you directions to an as yet undecided place and will distract you from trying to determine the nature of the true problem.

Instead ask...
"What is the true problem in this situation?"

And the conscious analysis which should follow can help you discover what the essential elements might be. Later, meaningful ideas can be related to the discovered real problems for more beneficial resolutions.

...and the PROCESS begins

the Birth of a Problem

Solving problems is a universal occupation.
Small or large, personal or social, we are
all busy at one problem situation or another.
What to do to pass this course? Which subject
to choose for a project or term paper? What
to do tonight? Which color to select? How
to improve the back yard? Where to get money?
Which city to begin looking for a job? How to
stop pollution? Where to begin on the task of
designing a safer bicycle?

Situations which present problem-solving
activity do not always arrive pre-digested and
clearly presented for easy management. Instead,
they more than likely will be tangled within
other situations; disguised or innocent-appearing
and locked inside some emotional distress or
values conflict or perhaps stemming from some
difficulty with the way things work (or don't
work). Because of this, it is possible to
spend much time and energy trying to untangle
the pre-problem mess before ever getting onto
the initial acceptance stage.

Although problems surround us in many apparently
different forms, it is only their specific
situations which differ. The process for
resolving them remains the same...they must all
be understood and the understanding must be
turned into action (analysis-synthesis). The
details of that process include decisions
regarding depth of personal involvement within
either portion. That's the big difference.
Some problems seem impossible to solve; others
don't seem like problems at all.

Some problems confront us as we move toward goals:

> "I took the course to learn about chemistry and now I've also got to learn how to think."

> "I wanted to fix the car by the weekend, but I can't get the parts I need."

 Some problems come to us from others:

> "You'll just have to postpone your trip until these additional drawings are completed."

> "I'm really sorry about your car. I just couldn't see it as I backed up my truck."

 And some problems come from within:

- from ethics:

> "I've got to do something about my urge to goof off when I should be studying."

> "I promised to go to work on the same night of the long-awaited concert. What to do?"

- from discontent:

> "I've got to find a way to add life to my dreary work area."

> "There must be some way to improve the nutritional content of foods in the cafeteria."

- from a human need for achievement, praise, love, etc.:

> "I'm going to learn how to build a sauna."

> "I plan to become an expert in Sherlock Holmes' mysteries before next summer."

> "I'll paint the guest room to show how much I care."

which specific situation bothers you?

Introduction to ACCEPTANCE

"Relax and enjoy it"

The first ENERGY STATE encountered in the
design process is ACCEPTANCE.

To accept the problem means you assume
responsibility for it. And in order to do
that you voluntarily agree to adapt your personal needs so that they coincide, at least in
part, with the as yet unknown requirements of
the problem. In short, ACCEPTANCE is an act
of self-giving. It makes sense to consider
it carefully to decide whether or not your
involvement is both possible and practical.
So many people dive into problems with the
"best of intentions" only to discover part way
into the fray that they either do not have the
interest or the qualifications to continue to
the end.

Conscious acceptance helps you determine whether
or not you have the ability, the time and the
energy and to decide whether or not the problem
in question will fit into your existing
schedule of priorities. It is always more
difficult to back out of a problem after
committing yourself to its resolution than it
is to reject participation from the outset.
Some degree of self-motivation will be required
throughout any effort. That is simply a matter
of control and persistence. But, if you find
yourself having to manufacture interest in a
problem over and above normal self-motivation,
it should be clear that you are not "in tune"
with that problem and should drop it as soon as
it is practicable.

36

Depth of involvement is the best measure of
acceptance. When the problem and the problem-
solver become synonymous, as though they are
one, a deep involvement will be perceived.
You will give off "acceptance vibes";
everyone will be aware of your involvement.

Acceptance is the first major Energy State
along our problem-solving journey. We must
pass through this state successfully before we
can logically enter into many of the "states"
beyond it...a continuing requirement throughout
the journey. Although it is possible to physically
go on (to have a little fun and also learn some
important skills, facts and attitudes) without
deeply accepting the task of solving a problem
situation, it should be clear that deeper
learning and greater pleasure can only be
gotten via whole-hearted acceptance of the
situation in question.

Language Guide For Acceptance

To accept the Problem Situation is often stated as:
*to declare initial objectives
*to buy the problem
*to give yourself to the situation
*to assign autonomy to the problem
*to value the project greater than self
*to assume the responsibility of the problem
*to dedicate your time and energy
*to believe in the problem
*to pledge self to the problem
*to take the problem into yourself
*to promise to resolve the problematic condition
*to alter your list of priorities
*to give consent or approval to solving the
  problem
*to confirm and marry the situation
*to make the problem a part of yourself
*to make the problem synonymous with yourself
*to establish motives; become motivated

What does "to accept the problem" mean to you?

Methods for Acceptance

Here is a group of methods which might help you to begin your problem-solving journey with a deeper acceptance.

1. Ad Valorem Method
2. Personal Priorities Matrix
3. What's in it for me? Method
4. Self-Hypnotism Method
5. Conformity Method
6. Give it up Method
7. Who's in Charge? Method
8. I am Responsible Method
9. I am the Victim Method
10. Analogy Acceptance Method
11. Put Yourself on the Spot or False Pride Method
12. Declaration of Acceptance Method
13. I am Famous and Fortunate Method
14. What's Holding you Back Method
15. Stanislavski Method

ways to get started

1 AD VALOREM

Generally you get out of something in proportion to what you put into the thing; i.e., your mood or frame of emotions regarding things usually determines your enjoyment of things. For example: an inexpensive trinket that you might ordinarily ignore can begin to take on a higher value if it is the gift of a loved one. By association, the trinket increases its importance to perhaps that of a far more expensive piece of jewelry. Likewise, a notebook which has been personalized with carefully drawn, colored illustrations or with other relevant notes or details will increase the value of a project or course of study for its owner.

In the same way, problem situations can have their values increased by finding ways to upgrade any apparently low worth that strange or unfriendly situations may present...helping to increase your interest by increasing their importance to you. How could you make your situation more valuable?

Before intending to spend a chunk of your life solving a problem, check to see how that problem relates to your other life objectives and abilities.

38

Since acceptance means to assume the responsibility for something, it's a good idea, before the fact, to see whether or not you have room in your life for one more responsibility.

2 PERSONAL PRIORITIES MATRIX

Using a simple matrix, compare what you expect the problem will demand of your time and energy against the existing demands you have facing you (A matrix is a grid of squares.)

EXAMPLES
1. List the demands of the problem: Cost in money, time, stress, etc., and place the list on the horizontal columns of the matrix.
2. List the existing demands on your life on the vertical columns of the matrix (jobs, duties, etc.)
3. Compare the two columns, using an "X" to denote conflicts. Overly conflicting situations suggest that the problem does not fit your current life-style or that those things which currently take up your time could stand to be altered or eliminated.

This method gives a brief overall graphic model of the entire problematic situation which faces you and also provides a clue to your expected chances for solving it. Remember, don't get in over your head!

3 WHAT'S IN IT FOR ME?

What do you expect to benefit from your involvement? How much do you expect to be paid? Make a list of all the benefits which may be gained if you do choose to accept the responsibility for the problem which faces you. Be as selfish as you like. Remember that direct benefits, such as immediate pleasures, recognition, money, property and gifts are more satisfying than indirect ones. And don't forget to include the possible development or improvement of skills, gaining new knowledge and general attitudes which could be useful for other situations in life. In the end the benefits should outweigh the costs to you in order to make your investment of energy worth your effort.

If you do choose to accept the problem, carry your "payment" schedule along with you. It will be a constant incentive to persist if the going gets tough later on.

39

4 SELF-HYPNOTISM

This is a method for talking yourself into and through a problem-solving situation.

Go to a quiet place. Take a walk alone or shut out the world of people and problems in some way. Clear your mind of everything. Relax. Get very still and try to shake off all awareness of your environment. Your body should feel first heavy, then numb and then asleep. Don't allow anything to distract you from concentrating on nothingness.

When you are relaxed and almost on the verge of sleep, change your concentration from the void to the positive aspects of the problem situation. Think how good it will be when it is solved. Think of how exciting it is to be involved in such an important task and of the feeling of well-being you will have as you continue to work at that task. Remind yourself of one of the rewards for solving problems and then slowly wake yourself up again to the task. The entire process could take as little as five minutes or as long as one hour and can be repeated as often as necessary throughout the course of your problem. (Also see SIDE TRIPS for more on this method.)

If you are active at the outset of a problem, ride with the feeling.

5 CONFORMITY

The quickest and easiest way to become a part of something is to become as much as possible like that thing. Conform to the problem and you will begin to indicate all of the necessary behavior of acceptance. Wear the clothes of the problem; talk its language. Go to its favorite places; eat its food; sing its songs; carry its mottos. Be as much like the problem as you can.

When your friends begin to mention how much like your problem you have become, you will be well on your way to the next energy state.

Acceptance demands freedom from pride, adaptability, tolerance and self-motivation.

6 GIVE IT UP

Zen philosophy suggests that the attainment of a thing requires the giving up of that thing. This means if you want something you must stop concentrating on having that thing and the fact that you want it (the product orientation) and begin concentrating on what the thing is and on what must be done to get it (process orientation).

EXAMPLES

1. If your problem-situation requires you to get $1,000, "give it up." Instead, get involved with things which earn money like turning your hobby into a profit or getting into some money-producing interest. By thus "giving it up," you will probably end up with more than the mere $1,000 you had as an initial product intention or goal.
2. If your problem is to design a house, "give it up." Get into what makes a house satisfying and you will soon be designing a good house.

7 WHO'S IN CHARGE

There are two profound choices in life: to accept things as they exist or to accept the responsibility for changing them. We control our own environment in accord with our number of decisions to accept change to meet our needs. The moment we recognize a situation in need of improvement (something which controls us need-lessly) we are faced with choosing to live with it consciously or to accept the task of removing it as a control over our life.

One method to encourage acceptance, therefore, is to constantly remind yourself of "Who's in charge" of your life and to realize that freedom and self-control only accrue to those who accept the responsibility to change your life in terms of your intentions.

Half-hearted acceptance produces half-way solutions.

8 I AM RESPONSIBLE

The work and responsibilities which go with everyday small problems are easy to handle compared to those which accompany heavy social, humanistic or ecological situations. Just to get the feeling of how simple it is to carry the load of your problem, try playing some of those "heavy" roles. Make it as real a game as you can, and imagine all the headaches of a really tough situation.

Think of a job you wouldn't have on a bet... and take it on (in your imagination) to find out how simple your task is by comparison.

41

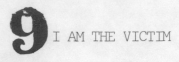

9 I AM THE VICTIM

One method for developing a strong motivation
to solve the situation which faces you is to
imagine becoming the victim of all of the worst
things that could happen if the situation were
not solved.

EXAMPLES:

Suppose you want to accept the problem of
helping others in your town see the pollution
caused by burning trash and paper in home
fireplaces.

Imagine that 50,000 new homes are being
built with large fireplaces. Next, imagine
that trash collectors go on strike and every
new fireplace becomes a home incinerator for
burning trash and garbage. Imagine the sky
to be much smoggier than it is, etc. Keep
on this line of attack and you will build a
strong case in your mind for immediate action.
The worse you imagine the consequences, the
greater your involvement might become.

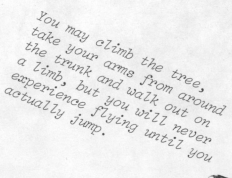

10 ANALOGY ACCEPTANCES

When you have trouble with accepting some
problem situation, try thinking of ways in
which other people or things accept their
situations.

Then, through the analogy, perhaps you too can
accept your problem. You will be less prejudiced
if you pick a subject very different from your
own.

You may climb the tree,
take your arms from around
the trunk and walk out on
a limb, but you will never
experience flying until you
actually jump.

EXAMPLES

How does a toaster accept toast?
It makes it easy by providing a large push bar.
It takes it in completely.
It concentrates all of its energy on all
   surfaces of the toast.
It accepts different sizes and types of
   bread (within limits).
It never half-toasts unless it is broken, etc.

FURTHER EXAMPLES:

How does a door accept people?
How does a cat accept affection?
How does a tree accept winter?

11 PUT YOURSELF ON THE SPOT OR FALSE PRIDE

A technique often used to bolster will-power is to put yourself in a position of "losing face" if you don't go through with your claims. This method is a form of witness gathering whereby you make public declarations in the presence of people expected to hold you to your word. Thus chained to your task, you dare not quit.

EXAMPLE:

Tell five (5) people who are high on your list of important people about your intentions concerning the acceptance of your problem. State realistic "due-dates." Tell them that you mean business. Get yourself really "in deep" so it will be difficult to back out and you will force yourself to persist until you achieve your goal.

Our abilities to accept things differ. All problems are relative and personal things.

12 DECLARATION OF ACCEPTANCE

This is a variation of the previous method. It took great courage for the signers of the Declaration of Independence to put their names on a document which subverted their existing government. But their signatures attest to their full acceptance of backing up their beliefs. Perhaps such a document could help you to accept the responsibility of your problem situation.

EXAMPLE:

Write down why you believe that the solving of your problem is a viable way to expend your energies. Write it like a long motto. Make it large and clear and hang it up near you so that you and others can see it. Maybe you could Xerox copies and give them to ten (10) people who you think might be interested.

13 WHAT'S HOLDING YOU BACK?

The four main causes of non-acceptance (other than physical disability or lack of skill) are:

1. It seems like or actually will be punishment to do it.
2. It seems like or actually will be more beneficial to do something else.
3. The relevance of doing it is not understood.
4. There are other problems which come before or stand in the way.

To overcome these factors, it is first necessary to identify which of them are operative. Then it becomes a matter of setting up a plan of contingency management...i.e., finding ways to either reward or punish yourself for desirable or undesirable behavior. By giving yourself the authority to control your behavior in a conscious way, what you do and why you do it becomes important in a general sense.

14 STANISLAVSKI

Constantin Stanislavski, the Russian director and dramatic coach who is noted for his METHOD principles, provides some choice advice relative to getting involved with a task. He writes of being "ceremonious," of turning the task into a memorable event...of treating the situation with reverence and respect. He suggests being light-headed and bouyant regarding the situation... as if it had almost magical qualities...of flowing with the situation...allowing it to carry you instead of imagining to confront it or of dealing with it as a manipulator. He admonishes us to drop our preconcepts and generalized opinions of the situation and to meet it with openness and love.

It is a hopeless mistake to wait until you have a sure-fire solution before declaring your acceptance of solving a problem. With such an attitude you enter problem-solving processes with all decisions previously made. You will have no alternatives.

15 THE HABIT BREAKER

Since acceptance calls for adaptation to new situations, the things between you and accepting your problem are your habits. You don't want to change from what you are doing or what you thought you would be doing. You resent being "told" what to do by the problem.

Acceptance is like signing a contract to buy an old house. You simply commit yourself to get involved with a lot of work in exchange for the security of having a place of your own.

The mere act of beginning a project increases your chances of completing it and builds confidence in your ability to go on to the end.

After you make an assessment of your long-range goals and decide that the problem does fit into your life, you then have to break those habits which tend to keep you outside of the problem by painstakingly forming a set of new ones.

RECIPE:

Make a list of the reasons why you don't want to face the problem or why you are afraid to face the problem. The list will probably describe, in other terms, all of those habits which currently make your non-accepting life-style comfortable.

Next, take the items, one by one, and consciously attempt to break them by replacing them with new accepting behaviors. It will be difficult and exciting since it will open new doors into the problem for you to enter it more easily.

EXAMPLE:

I don't want to accept this problem because:
1. It will keep me from seeing my friend.
2. My money is already committed.
3. The problem seems complex and I've always disliked big "head" trips, etc.

HABIT BREAKERS:
1. Allow this to be a test of your friend's understanding and tolerance.
2. Reorganize your finances and payment schedule.
3. Take a chance on seeing if the problem is really as complex as it appears or if the block is in your mind.

...and then, sometimes acceptance can come only after acquiring some information. Go on to ANALYSIS and see if you can learn to get into the problem just a little bit more in that way.

Travel Guides for Acceptance

Fromm, Erich, Avon
ESCAPE FROM FREEDOM

Mager, Robert, et al, Fearon
ANALYZING PERFORMANCE PROBLEMS

Schoonmaker, Alan, Harper & Row
A STUDENT'S SURVIVAL MANUAL
Esp. "Opportunities Analysis Questionnaire"

Stanislavski, Constantin, Theatre Arts
CREATING A ROLE

45

Introduction
to ANALYSIS

Once deeply inside of any single thing, you find yourself automatically into all things.

Getting to know more about the problem situation
and clarifying all that you already know about
it are the two basic tasks of ANALYSIS, the next
logical problem-solving stage. By traveling
through the ACCEPTANCE stage you may have already uncovered many new possibilities and some
of what you know (since it is improbable to
accept anything you knew nearly nothing about).
When a deep involving acceptance calls for an
intense ANALYSIS you will begin to see the many
apparent interrelationships between your subject-
situation and other things. It is then that
the information gathering, listing, sorting and
comparing task may seem endless; when time
limits and constraints of information quantity
and type must be set to avoid over-study and
avoidance of the resolution you set out to
achieve.

ANALYSIS can appear to be a boring and dry (but necessary) stop along the way toward more exciting states if it is not understood as the equally exciting state where the bulk of your learning takes place...that state where your existing knowledge regarding the subject is revealed and made orderly and where new knowledge comes easily because what you already know is clearly available for relationship.

Like the other states ANALYSIS, once consciously applied, may continually gnaw at your conscience throughout the process; urging you to circle back for a few more bits of information; leaving you rarely satisfied to have discovered enough.

Language Guide for Analysis

<u>To Analyze a problem is often stated as:</u>
to take the problem apart
to research and question a subject
to discover interrelations and patterns
to examine parts in relation to whole
to dissect or decompose the problem
to gather facts and opinions
to find out about the problem
to get familiar with the problem
to compare your problem situation with other
   situations
to question or interrogate the problem
to spread the problem out before yourself
to sort, sequence or order the problem
to classify the elements of the situation
to search for insight within the problem

What does "to analyze the problem" mean to you?

The two basic analytical methods are: 1) to question and 2) to compare; i.e., to seek information through active curiosity and to relate one thing to other things to determine interrelatedness. All analytical methods are variations on these two prototypes.

Methods for Analysis

1. The Basic Question Method
2. The Pack Rat Method
3. Synectics/Forced Relationship Methods
4. "Back to the Sun" Method
5. Attribute Listing Method
6. "Record All You Know About It" Method
7. "What Have Others Done" Method
8. Analysis Models Method
9. Morphological Method
10. Matrix Method
11. "Search for Patterns" Method
12. The Expert Consultant Method
13. Expanding Objectives Method
14. The Idea-Dump Method
15. The Sensitivity Game
16. Squeeze and Stretch Method

ways for getting to know the problem

1 THE BASIC QUESTIONS

The mere asking of a question calls for courage; however, asking a question is all that is necessary to enter the state of Analysis. It is the universal method for finding out about something. It means throwing off fear and pride to determine what, why, where, when and who. The basic questions tend to be:

Who can help me solve this problem?
What has already been tried to solve this problem?
Are there books or references available?
What are my resources and what is required?
Where can information be found?
What is the total scope or "world" of this problem?
Which limits can I control and which are fixed?
What is allowed and what is ruled out?
Can the rules be changed?

Analysis never stops unless you stop it because getting to know about something is an endless process. Remember that all things are related to everything else. Set a time limit on your analysis phase.

48

THE PACK RAT

The Pack Rat, like the crow, gathers things around it which have attracted its attention for one reason or another. Analysis, handled in the style of the Pack Rat, is a random and haphazard thing. To deliberately pursue analysis that way would suggest that time and energy expense were of no importance. But much information can still be gathered this way.

And for short designated periods of time, during the course of a usually limited situation, the Pack Rat Method can also be useful.

EXAMPLE: For a half an hour each day during the course of your problem, go somewhere new and bring back something new to your problem "nest." Go to a new room in the library, see a new "consultant," walk into a strange laboratory, visit another problem situation in progress, etc. Don't be too concerned about categorization; that can happen later. Just be a Pack Rat and bring back something which "attracts" you.

Afterward you can make a game of relating the bits of your "collection" to your problem situation while remembering that all things are interrelated.

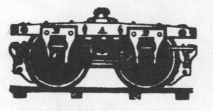 SYNECTICS/FORCED RELATIONSHIP

Gaining deeper insights and new perspectives are both attempts to see things in ways that you have not seen them before. Synectics (see SIDE TRIPS) and Forcing Relationships are two methods for reaching such new views.

Synectics asks, "How is this thing like that thing?" using the similarities uncovered to provide new viewpoints of those items being compared.

Forced Relationship asks, "What would result if I combined or joined this thing to that thing?"; the conclusions providing deeper insight into the roles of both "components."

EXAMPLE: Analyze a fireplace.
1. How is a fireplace like a breakfast cereal?
   They both provide heat by distributing energy.
   They are both involved with fuel consumption, etc.

None are so blind as those who refuse to see. Analysis also suggests that we question and compare with all our senses.

2. What would result if a fireplace were joined to a table?

   A table on which you could cook; the hearth could be a coffee table, and etc.

   A stove top of Pyrex on which to both cook and eat or a fireplace which transmits radiant heat through a glass hood.

Every answer gets you one notch deeper into understanding the problem and its potentials.

4 BACK TO THE SUN

Since all physical things are reducible to primary energy sources, you can analyze things by tracing their "history" of processing back to their natural resource states and ultimately to the Sun as the source of all energy. This method can become a game of trying to find the largest list of "historical" points in the process.

EXAMPLE: <u>Look at your shoe.</u> What do you see?

Response: I see leather, rubber, strings, nails, grommets, polish, thread, etc. And for each of these, I can trace a process back to natural resources and the Sun.

<u>Nails</u>
Hammer
Forge
Wire Spool
Steel
Drawing
Pittsburgh
Shipping
Minnesota
Iron
Fossil
Deposits

<u>Polish, etc.</u>
Application
Coloring
Container
Mixing
Trucking
Petroleum
Chemicals
Fossil Deposits

<u>Leather</u>
Texturing
Coloring
Holes Punched
Cut Out
Tannery
Slaughter-
house
Trucking
Ranch
Grass, Feed

<u>Strings</u>
Plastic Tips
Woven Fabric
Coloring
Fibre
Woven
Fibre
Spinning
Fibre
Drawing
Fibre
Synthesizing
Plastic
Petroleum
Chemicals
Fossil Deposits

<u>Rubber</u>
Stamps
Mold
Heel Factory
Shipping
Raw Latex
Processing
Rubber Plant
Rubber Tree

50

5 ATTRIBUTE LISTING

Attributes are the different categories into which all of the physical, psychological and social characteristics of things can be placed. Getting to know something better involves discovering the unique attributes of that thing.

By making a list of the attributes of the subject being analyzed you assemble the parts for both a general and specific view of the "world" of that subject.

SOME EXAMPLES OF ATTRIBUTES ARE:
 Physical (color, weight, mass, speed, odor, size, structure, order, etc.)
 Psychological (appearance, perceptual stimulus, symbolism, etc.)
 Social (group approvals, taboos, responsibilities, politics, etc.)
 Others (cost, function, durability, ecological connection, time, etc.)

Note: Attributes can also be considered as problem variables which are dependent (on other attributes) or independent. To know which is which will often be helpful in the determination of component importances at later problem-solving stages.

The more you attempt to see inside of things, the more you develop your power of insight.

6 PUT DOWN ALL YOU KNOW

We begin all analysis with a question. The first question is the hardest but one question leads to another.

Most of us know much more about things than we give ourselves credit for knowing. We may back off when asked what we know about something we imagine not to have examined carefully before, only to discover, upon examination, that we already knew much of it. Let someone ask us if we know the names of 25 wines and we'd probably say "no." Then, seeing a list of 50 wine names, we'd probably recognize them all and say, "Oh, I knew those!" But by then it is too late! Too bad!

This method is about writing down all that you know about the subject in question. You must force it out of yourself, though, because you are naturally reluctant to write down the "obvious." In short, most of what you know is locked inside as potential awaiting your authority for release.

For example, by "talking things over" with a friend you'd be surprised at all the two of you know about things. Writing them down or putting them on tape and then writing them down is all-important. So get a pad and pencil and sit down alone (or with a friend) and start writing down an outline of all you already do know about your problem situation...start with the "obvious."

A wide-awake young traveler can surpass the overconfident tour leader in the gathering of information about a place.

7 WHAT HAVE OTHERS DONE

Although revolutionary developments which deny history are possible, it is evolutionary growth that is probable. Both you and your situation are parts of long chains of interrelated situations over time. This commonly used method deals with the critical examination of the solutions which others have applied to solve problems similar to yours.

Once again, make a list. This time your list is of previous solutions. After each entry, include some critical evaluative comments about each one. The library is a good place to begin because most important or ingenious solutions are recorded in magazines, journals and in books.

8 ANALYSIS MODELS

Another way to get to know about a subject or situation is to build a model of it. A simulation will help you see what not to do when you actually build it. Models can take many forms. Model trains, airplanes and houses are just one kind of model. They are very helpful in visualizing form, color, proportional relationships, etc. But models do not have to be three dimensional miniatures of your intended objectives.

Other ways to model your intended objectives include full-size prototypes, charts, statistical graphs, pattern assemblies, biological analogies, perhaps even an ant farm could successfully model a social system, etc. For instance, the best model for analyzing the problem of writing a letter to Mom might easily be writing the letter to Mom. If it doesn't work out, it's simple enough to start over.

Nothing important will be wasted, and some parts may be reusable if you decide to scrap the first attempt. For more complex problems, where people and resources become important, such an approach could get out of hand and quickly become irresponsible. At those times more efficient models, such as charts of interrelationships, time-energy comparisons, logistical and statistical methods, would be more practical.

Since "waking up" to the existence of problems within the problem often comes only after doing it wrong the first time, a bag of different model techniques is handy to carry along on problem-solving journeys.

9 MORPHOLOGICAL

One kind of model found to be useful in visualizing "whole worlds of potentials" of things is the "morphological" model, a simple way of organizing the attributes or components of a subject and for dealing with them as interrelationships.

Follow this simple procedure:
1. List all the problem attributes (variables)
2. Categorize the attributes making separate lists for each category
3. Systematically determine the combinations by taking one attribute from each list and finding out about that particular combination of parts.

The 3-D Morphology uses solid geometric forms (cube, rectangular solid, or polygonal solid) to help visualize the complete possibilities or potentials of a subject by examining all the relationships found at each intersection or "cell" formed by the meetings of attributes within the model.

Don't begin your analytic search with a ready-made answer. Use the search to determine the answer. A fixed mind is closed to discovery.

Seek out some of the "dirty jobs" in analysis. Truth often hides in the corners.

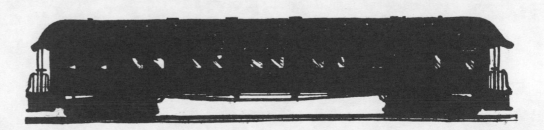

10 MATRIX

A matrix is like the mileage chart found on most road maps. On these charts you see the names of cities in vertical and horizontal lines at the top and side of a grid. At each intersection of the grid you find a number which corresponds to the distance between the two cities involved. When a city connects with itself there is a dot or a blank to symbolize "no relationship."

Similarly, a matrix can help clarify relationships between elements or attributes of a problem situation. By placing variables, attributes or limitations of a problem on <u>both axes</u> of a matrix, you are able to plot the interrelationship between each of them. In this way you can systematically determine which of them are most dependent or independent. (Note! A numerical rating system can add more precision to this method.) Draw a grid. Place the problem components at both the top and side of the grid and start determining relationships. You will have to work out a system for dealing consistently with all the decisions you must make in the matrix.

Get your questions out of your mind by asking them out loud and by writing them down. Questioning is a learned skill and is developed through practice.

11 SEARCH FOR PATTERNS

Within every problem there can be found smaller problems or sub-situations, and for each of those solutions might also be found. Problem solving usually consists of resolving lots of small situations leading toward a collective end or goal. The search for patterns (or previous and/or typical solutions to individual parts of the problem) is another useful method. Clearly, the more patterns which can be collected, the greater will be the 'vocabulary' of the "language" used in solving particular problems.

FOR EXAMPLE: In the problem of how to improve travel by air, we might find that one typical sub-situation is too-great distances between cities and airports. One workable response to this situation has been helicopter service to and from airports and downtown centers. This pattern then becomes a part of a larger language of patterns to be compiled for use in other air-traveler problems.

Patterns can be found wherever previous experience or a collection of bits and pieces exists.

Analysis means looking into places you haven't looked before or seeing familiar things in new ways. Going over the same things in the same ways teaches nothing new.

12 THE EXPERT CONSULTANT

When the going gets tough and a problem leans heavily on your back, being able to rely on an expert consultant can save the day. Professional diagnosticians (physicians, lawyers, architects, etc.) suggest that you consider their services as "preventative" measures instead of only when "it's almost too late." This method therefore suggests calling in an expert before, instead of only after, the fact of acting on your problem. They may be real or imaginary.

TRY THIS: In your mind (or via books, tapes or even reality) call in the one or two people you think would be most helpful to your excursion through the Energy State of Analysis. If your problem deals with religion, you could call in Jesus Christ or Buddha to sit and discuss the situation with you. Anyone is available to be your consultant (without charge) if only you will call them into your mind. A good beginning might be to ask, "I wonder what _____ would have to say about this problem?" Who will you ask to help you?

Always keep your recording tools close at hand while passing through the Energy State of Analysis. You'll need plenty of references later on which can be best collected and organized right now.

13 EXPANDING OBJECTIVES

We enter the analytic state by having already accepted certain basic intentions or objectives. As we follow the course outlined by those objectives, we will probably discover new territory in the line of our desires. Clearly, the analysis state can be broadened and made more meaningful as a journey if we continually attempt to expand and to clarify those objectives which we use to guide us.

When a new discovery is fed back to broaden our objectives, then the newly broadened objectives will guide us into ever new territory as in a chain reaction. In the end, those objectives which have been expanded as far as possible become the specifications for the improved performance you conclude as the resolution to your problem. The more you expand and clarify them, the closer you get to the realization of the solution itself. (Also see SIDE TRIPS for more on "how to clarify objectives" by making them "measurable.")

14 THE IDEA-DUMP

Sometimes an idea can be our worst enemy, especially if it blocks our thinking of other alternatives at the analysis stage.

If we enter into problem situations carrying an "ace-in-the-hole," no matter how much we "say" we are going to analyze and "be objective" about this thing, we still know that we don't have to work too hard at it because there is always one way out of the dilemma and we have that way hidden in our pocket.

The idea-dump method asks you to get all of your "aces" out front from the beginning so that they don't block your path through analysis. Once out front, those ideas can be critically examined by you and others and along with the criticism will come deeper understanding.

EXAMPLE:
1. Search your mental "pockets" for ideas before you enter the State of Analysis. Cleanse your mind.
2. Share your ideas with others. Ask them to tell you why they will or won't work.
3. Use the results to lead you into further research.
4. Save all usable ideas and parts of ideas for use later after the problem is defined.

Don't let the need to make records get in the way. If your eye is glued to the camera you may miss seeing the whole scene. Record with the senses (to be transcribed later on) as well as with equipment.

15 The SENSITIVITY GAME

Imagination rarely matches reality. Before reaching sixteen years old, we tend to touch, taste, smell and listen to everything strange to us. That's how we learn and those who sense the most usually learn the most. After that, society programs us to keep our senses "under control" and to turn our senses off.

If you want to find out more about something, it's a good plan to get very close to it. Put a felt pen into your mouth and at once you become aware of the taste of the ingredients of ink. Touch a snake and you probably dis- cover it to be much less slimy than you thought. Touch a fish and you may find it to be twice as slimy as you thought.

This method is a socially reactionary game. It simply asks that the first thing you do when involved in analysis is to check it out via the senses. Examine it with your finger. Feel its surface and take its temperature. Smell it and compare its odors with others. Taste it if possible. Record the sounds it emits. Look it over carefully.

Remember that day when you petted a horse for the first time how different it was from what your imagination and anxiety had previously led you to expect. Touching made all the difference in how you now understand horses.

16 SQUEEZE AND STRETCH

Discovering "whole worlds" and "specific contexts" of your problems is another way of defining analysis. You have to "stretch" problems out to see just how much there is inside and how all of its parts relate to other things in the environment. And you have to "squeeze" them down to their essential elements in order to view them in the correct proportional relationship to that same total environment.

Squeezing and stretching becomes a handy method for analysis.

To STRETCH out a problem situation and discover its parts, ask a chain of questions beginning with "what?".

EXAMPLES
Q. What is this problem about? ANSWER: Judo.
Q. What is "Judo" all about? ANSWER: Physical efficiency.
Q. What is "Physical Efficiency" all about? ANSWER: Finding the optimal use of body movement.

To SQUEEZE a problem down to its essentials, ask a chain of questions beginning with "why?".

EXAMPLES
Q. Why am I doing this? ANSWER: I want to.
Q. Why do I want to? ANSWER: It makes me happy.
Q. Why will it make me happy?, etc.

The things we lose are often found in unexpected places. If you are looking for information... like anything else, try looking in the unexpected places, too.

57

Travel Guides for Analysis

Alexander, Christopher J., Harvard
NOTES ON THE SYNTHESIS OF FORM

Gordon, William J. J., Collier
SYNECTICS

Jones, Christopher, Wiley
DESIGN METHODS

Mager, Robert, Fearon
GOAL ANALYSIS

Parnes, Sidney J., Scribners
CREATIVE BEHAVIOR WORKBOOK and
CREATIVE BEHAVIOR GUIDEBOOK

Simon, Herbert A., Wiley
MODELS OF MAN

Stevens, John O., Real People Press
AWARENESS: Exploring Experimenting Experiencing

_____, Simon & Shuster
THE WAY THINGS WORK, Vols. 1 and 2.

Introduction to DEFINITION

Every country has its own version
of vegetable soup. The names are
different but the stuff is the same.

Making statements and restatements of definitions
for problem situations seems to be the intellec-
tual task of our species. Whether at the
beginning, during the process, or at its conclusion, we invariably work toward getting closer
to the truth of things with each such statement.

Our degree of comprehension and clarity of
definition at any point in time is dependent
on our insight and our insight grows out of
experience. These "concepts," as they are
often called, develop and change as experience
builds. Thus there will probably be as many
different meanings given to any one thing as
there are people or groups to provide them;
the uniqueness of each of our problem definitions being the prime expression of our individuality or personal philosophy.

Now, at this third stage of the DESIGN PROCESS,
we can build a bridge between the analyzed
facts and attributes we have just discovered
and the alternatives/decision-making phase
which is to follow. We can "conceive" the
statement or set of guidelines which expresses
our new comprehension of the problem now
analyzed; a statement which, like the "eye of
a needle," will provide alignment for all
decisions after the fact. We have reached the
point of declaration.

Our definition becomes the filter for future
decisions regarding the problem. And our
solution, in the end, will become a physical
translation of this statement.

Later on, if we discover the situation to mean
different or expanded things, we can always
change our mind and try it differently the next
time around.

We begin each problem with some basic "definition," which is the sum of our experience to
that moment; what we think the problem means
as we attempt to describe it at that beginning
level of understanding. Then as we progress
through the process, our understanding of the
situation develops into progressively clearer
statements until at last we can say the problem
is understood. If the situation occurs again,
we either apply the same hard-won previous
definition to the new situation or we begin
anew, with a higher level of understanding,
prepared to progress to even greater levels of
understanding.

Language Guide for Definition

Your definition of a situation can be thought
of in many ways. Here are some of the popular
ones:

*Your concept or attitude about the problem

*An expression of your values regarding
 the problem situation

*The truth as far as you know it at
 the time

*Your current understanding of the
 problem

*A declaration of what you believe;
 your attitude

*Your clearest intention; your ultimate
 goal and the objectives designated to
 reach it

*Your closest verbal analogy of the
 situation

*Your expectations

*Your index for decision-making; the
 mold or die through which all your
 decisions will pass

*Your underlying or foremost meaning
 of the problem

*Your performance specifications for
 the problem resolution

How do you refer to the definition statement?

DEFINITION IS:

*A clarification of objectives
*A "Eureka" statement
*An essential statement (essence)
*A temporal statement on the path to truth
*Directions for action
*A distillation of subjective and
 objective responses
*A transformance of facts into guidelines
*Design objectives
*The dust particle around which the
 snowflake is formed
*Halfway to the solution
*Developing conceptual guidelines

the BRIDGE between Analysis & Synthesis

What does "to define the problem" mean to you?

Methods for Definition

1. "Whys" Guy Method
2. Essence-Finding by Matrix Method
3. The "Happiness is" Method
4. King-of-the-Mountain Method
5. Key-Word Distillery Method
6. Problems within Problems Method
7. Talk-it-out- Method
8. Essence-Finding by Consensus

1 "WHYS" GUY

Similar to the "stretch and squeeze" method experienced during our journey through analysis, this method also concentrates on what we already know and takes the "squeezing" part to a conclusion. If enough questions begin with the word "WHY" and if they are posed in a chain or series, a distillation of purpose begins to appear. That distilled purpose is the definition as it is envisioned by the problem solver who asks and answers the questions. The why-chain is a boiling-down process. It forces a constant clarification of objectives until an accepted essence statement is reached.

Try not to stop until at least ten (10) "why" questions have been answered and remember that it is better to be a Whys-Guy than never to have learned at all.

ways to determine a point of view

2 ESSENCE-FINDING BY MATRIX

In a simple matrix interrelationship, all of the attributes or components of a problem can be rated as to their dependence upon or independence from one another. By comparing them, one at a time, against each other we can also determine their degree of dependence or independence within the group as a whole. In this way the key variables are those elements which are ultimately determined to be most essential in the matrix.

Matrix interrelationships may be shuffled until groups or large patterns become clear. The large pattern relationships might then be studied as essential overall definition possibilities.

The basic definition-triggering question is "What is the real problem?" It may have to be asked many times before an acceptable response occurs.

Situations containing vast numbers of components can get to be quite difficult to manipulate requiring neat grids, strict adherence to notation and consistent criteria. Computer assistance might be called for in complex or very important situations.

3 HAPPINESS IS

Charles Schulz has given us a useful tool for unearthing definitions with his Happiness is cartoon book. To manufacture so many "defini- tions" for one word forces us to expand our limits of understanding of that word (or situation).

On a blackboard or large sheet of paper, list as many definitions as possible for the problem being studied. When you run out of energy, ask others to join in. Leave writing tools near the list so others will add definitions from time to time while you are away involved in other aspects of your research. You can also encourage every- one to treat the list as a graffiti game, allow- ing them to write down anything regarding the subject which might occur to them. It won't take long to collect many definitions.

4 KING-OF-THE-MOUNTAIN

In the children's game called King-of-the-Mountain, one player gets on top of something and the others try to undermine that position so that they might take it over. Each unsuccessful attempt to unseat the "king" strengthens the topmost position within the context of the game.

By using the same procedure, the elements, compon- ents, objectives or attributes of problems can be played against one another in order to determine a heirarchy of importances. By pitting them against each other, one at a time, and adding their total number of wins you will eventually be able to decide on the ones which are the strongest or which you most prefer over all others; the last one(s) you would be willing to discard in a show-down.

A second round might also be played. This time pit two players against other teams of two. Play this out until every pair has played against every other pair to determine if the "essential" ingredient (winner) is really a combination of concerns rather than simply one of them.

63

KEY-WORD DISTILLERY

This method consists of writing a long or composite statement describing the key issues of the problem and then extracting the key words or essentials from that statement.

DIRECTIONS:
Alone, or with a group, prepare a statement of what you believe to be important about the problem. In it, describe your objectives and all of the concerns which you feel to be important and/or clearly relevant. Do not stop until you are satisfied that the statement describes the problem clearly and broadly. Then go through the statement word by word, encircling all words or phrases which appear more essential than the others. Next, using only those key words and phrases, prepare another statement; a closer approximation of your definition of the problem. It may be necessary to rearrange the key words several times until a logical statement can be made from them. But via this deductive method, a series of disjointed facts can often be turned into a set of directions.

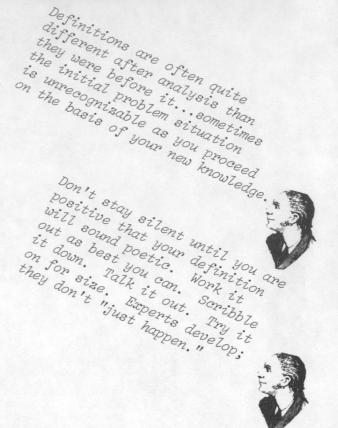

Definitions are often quite different after analysis than they were before it...sometimes the initial problem situation is unrecognizable as you proceed on the basis of your new knowledge.

Don't stay silent until you are positive that your definition will sound poetic. Work it out as best you can. Scribble it down. Talk it out. Try it on for size. Experts develop; they don't "just happen."

 PROBLEMS-WITHIN-PROBLEMS

Trying to improve situations and make things work better teaches us that inside of every problem situation, we can find many other sub-situations. Locating and resolving the key sub-problem as the generator of the whole situation is another way to describe the overall task of problem-solving.

Solve the sub-situation which is determined most crucial and you solve the entire situation.

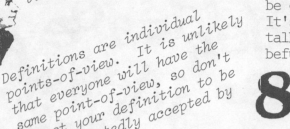

The secret to solving problems is to find the bridge between the way things are and the way you want them to become. That bridge is your definition; the link between the situation as already solved and its resolution as you envision it to be.

Definitions are individual points-of-view. It is unlikely that everyone will have the same point-of-view, so don't expect your definition to be whole-heartedly accepted by everyone.

7 TALK IT OUT

"Two heads are better than one" is the basis for this method which simply suggests that definitions come easier when you sit with a friend or consultant and "talk it out." The "it" we refer to is an acceptable definition of the problem at hand. You can attempt to discover, through discussion, what you agree upon as being the core of the situation. When more than two persons are involved in the session, an arbitrator should be chosen in order to avoid circular arguments. It's amazing to see how many definitions can be talked out of situations which seemed complex and befuddling only minutes before.

8 ESSENCE-FINDING BY CONSENSUS

The other person's problem never seems so heavy as your own. This makes it much easier to solve theirs rather than yours. Most everyone loves to offer opinions. It's an easy way to help out without spending much energy. So, if your problem calls for public approval, one way to get an acceptable definition for it is to allow the public to decide from among the choices you present to them. Ask a large number of people who will be affected by the solution to the situation to list their preferences in an order of importances. Glean an average or a workable compromise definition from the results. This method may also yield side benefits of additional insight and offers of assistance or experienced guidance.

Travel Guides for Definition

Kogan, Zuce, Z. Kogan
ESSENTIALS IN PROBLEM-SOLVING

Suzuki, D. T., Evergreen
AN INTRODUCTION TO ZEN BUDDHISM

Watts, Alan, Vintage
DOES IT MATTER?

Introduction to IDEATION

Having many ideas improves your chance for having a good idea when the time comes to decide on which one to use.

Searching for ideas is the next stage in the process. After you have defined your directions and your goal is clearly described it's time to generate options; alternative ways to achieve your goal.

Ideas are merely ways to get to where we want to go. That's all they are--no more, no less. If we have no place to go (poorly defined objectives), then ideas won't be of much help. Instead, they will just confuse the issue and keep us from concentrating on defining our goals.

If someone tosses an idea in your way before you have a "definite" direction you might be misled into taking a trip to someone else's destination instead of your own.

Getting all the ideas you could ever use is really not as tough as it may appear to many who "could have died" for just one "good idea." By having only a few idea-generating methods in your bag you can manufacture great quantities of ideas or ways to get where you want to go. By simply knowing where you want to go, you are at once in a position to find many, many ways to get there.

66

Language Guide for Ideation

Words don't have meanings: only people have meanings. They use words to express their meanings.

Don't worry about having lots of ideas from which to choose. You may as well choose from as wide a selection as possible.

Finding ideas for problems is often stated as:

To find the ways or means for reaching goals

To consider various strategies for reaching objectives

To generate alternate routes

To list all of the options or alternatives

To uncover the possible choices

To become aware of the different paths which might be taken

To make an index of potential plans for resolving the problem

To find the possibilities for action

What does searching for ideas mean to you?

Ideas are often somewhat misleadingly referred to as concepts, definitions and essentials in that their active content is suggestive of direction.

"I don't have any 'idea' (concept) about what she looks like."

"Now you get the idea (essence) of how to swim."

"All of a sudden my 'idea' (concept) became very clear."

Methods for Ideation

1. Brainstorming Method
2. Manipulative Verbs Method
3. Synectics (also see SIDE TRIPS)
4. "Tell me, stranger" Method
5. Go to the Library Method
6. Attribute Analogy Chains Method
7. "Get out of town" Method
8. Morphological Forced Connections Method
9. "Seeds of Ideas" Method

1 BRAINSTORMING

If you want ideas you've got to ask the right question which begs for ideas. "What are all the ideas for (solving the situation defined as----------?) is such a question...and is the basic key to Brainstorming.

Brainstorming is a universal problem-solving method and may be found useful in all stages of the process. However, generating alternatives is its basic use. It is useful because any group of 4 to 12 persons can quickly learn to manufacture scores of ideas for any problem situation in very short periods of time. (Fifty ideas in five minutes is not an unusually large number using brainstorming rules.)

The originator of brainstorming, Alex Osborn, lays down four requirements for all who parti- cipate in a session. Anyone can learn to apply them. The session is automatically retarded when the rules are ignored. They are:

1. Defer judgment. (Criticism comes afterward.)
2. Free-wheel. (Hang loose.)
3. Tag on. (Don't wait for an idea. Make another one out of the last one given by changing it in some way.)
4. Quantity is wanted. (Don't hold back for a minute.)

Suggestion: Learn to brainstorm with a small group before going it alone. The rules are easier to absorb into your behavior that way.

Restrict the sessions to about 5 minutes per subject and stop altogether after 15 or 20 minutes. A followup session, using the same participants on the next day, is a good way to pick up all of the "after-thoughts."

ways to broaden the field of choice.

Don't let ideas get in your way. If you have ways to go before you have a place to get to you may take a trip to nowhere.

2 MANIPULATIVE VERBS

Another Alex Osborn method uses a series of words to help us visualize our subject in unique (innovative) ways. The words (verbs) suggest manipulating the subject by changing its position or by altering its shape, function, size, etc. Using manipulative verbs can produce a series of ideas or unique views in a short time.

Osborn's verbs are:

```
Magnify     )-which if-----(Giant Garage
Minify      )-applied to a-(City Cabin
Rearrange   )-problem of---(Sleep In Kitchen
Alter       )-designing a--(Two Living Rooms
Adapt       )-new kind of--(Live in an Old Church
Modify      )-house might--(No Living Room
Substitute  )-yield:-------(Cave House
Reverse     )-------------(Live in the Garden
Combine     )-------------(Houseboat
```

The more ideas you gather, the better are your chances for having good ideas.

Other verbs which might also be used to produce unique views are:

Multiply	Distort	Fluff-up	Extrude
Divide	Rotate	By-pass	Repel
Eliminate	Flatten	Add	Protect
Subdue	Squeeze	Subtract	Segregate
Invert	Complement	Lighten	Integrate
Separate	Submerge	Repeat	Symbolize
Transpose	Freeze	Thicken	Abstract,
Unify	Soften	Stretch	etc.
Dissect			

Can you think of five (5) more?

3 SYNECTICS

Synectics is another general purpose technique. Basically it is a series of methods connected as a process; originated by William J. J. Gordon. (See SIDE TRIPS for a more complete description.) In the process of deriving new viewpoints, Synectics can also be useful for producing many ideas.

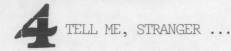

4 TELL ME, STRANGER ...

The problems easiest to solve usually belong to
the other person. The moment a problem becomes
"our problem," psychological barriers are set
up which make it seem to be a more complex
situation than it ever could have been before.
And because the "other person's" problems are so
simple to solve, we are always ready with an
idea for solving them.

Following that line of thinking, you might
benefit by asking someone outside of the common
problem limits for ideas. Since your problem
is not their problem, they may be ready with an
idea for you. The more casual the acquaintance,
the more likely it is that you will be given a
unique view. Close friends are often useless
when it comes to unique views because they assume
nearly the same personal feeling toward your
problem as you do.

EXAMPLE:
  You are a biology student trying to solve a
  problem regarding tide pool regeneration.
  You have defined your problem, stated your
  objectives and now need ideas for correcting
  the situation you have defined.

METHOD:
  Ask a sociology student. Ask an Environmental Technology instructor, walk through
  the Marine Sciences Building and ask the
  first five (5) people you meet. Write down
  all of the ideas, and bring them back to your
  problem.

*Freedom is often defined in terms
of the availability of options and
of the availability of alternatives.
choice; a variety of alternatives.
Yet how often do we begin a journey
thinking that there is but one way
to get to our destination.*

5 GO TO THE LIBRARY

Libraries have records of how your problem (or
at least a problem very much like yours) has
been solved in the past. You will find "how
to do it" books, magazines on current techniques
and practices and many new points of view regarding your situation. The Reference Librarian,
who may spend much time trying to help you, has
a knack for uncovering piles of information on
ways of doing things and other idea-spurring
materials. By writing down or Xeroxing all of
the ideas you find in the library, you will
develop a long list of alternatives in a
relatively short period.

6 ATTRIBUTE ANALOGY CHAINS

Ideas are often found in making analogies and the key to analogy is to force a relationship between two different things. You can find something alike about any two things. An obvious example is the fact that, when the Sun shines, it adds a similar component of yellow light to everything in its path, helping all of those things to find a harmonic connection.

If you use your list of problem attributes (from the Analysis stage) to guide you, chains of analogy ideas can be attached to each attribute.

FOR EXAMPLE:
In working on the problem of improving the design of a FIREPLACE, its basic attributes might be listed as:
NAME: FIREPLACE
FORM: GEOMETRIC, ANGULAR, CONICAL, ETC.
FUNCTION: HEAT ROOM, PSYCHOLOGICALLY
                  SOOTHING, ETC.
COLOR: BLACK, BRICK RED, ETC.
MATERIAL: STEEL, MASONRY, ETC.

to which we might tag on the following analogy-ideas:

NAME: COMBUSTION CHAMBER, TEA POT, AUTO
                  ENGINE, CIGARETTE LIGHTER, ETC.
FORM: ARCHITECTURAL CONSTRUCTIONS,
                  CRYSTALS, PRISMS, ETC.
FUNCTION: CAT ON LAP, ROBE, INTIMATE FRIEND,
                  ETC., ETC.

and produce the following alternative views:

CHANGE NAME TO ENERGY TRANSFORMER.
TRY FORMS WHICH ARE DERIVED FROM CRYSTAL
   STRUCTURES FOR BETTER RADIANT HEAT
   DISTRIBUTION.
USE BATH ROBE INSULATION PRINCIPLE TO CONSERVE
   HEAT, ETC.

7 GET OUT OF TOWN

Although discoveries can be made without leaving your own chair, the normal technique for unearthing new ways for doing things is to travel outside of your usual environment. This method suggests that travel can also take place in your mind. And that one way to find ideas is to mentally "get out of town." Allow yourself to take your problem to a new environment. If you live in Los Angeles and your problem concerns "clean air," take your problem to Tokyo and to Ankara

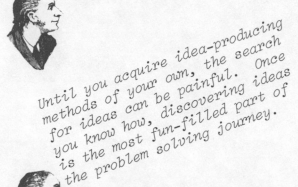

It makes no difference where ideas come from; it's what we do with them that matters. We don't have to justify our ideas but only our action and its consequences if we decide to follow one or more of them.

Until you acquire idea-producing methods of your own, the search for ideas can be painful. Once you know how, discovering ideas is the most fun-filled part of the problem solving journey.

and to London. Ask someone there (in your
mind) what they might do about your situation.
For instance, if you want ideas for a new market-
place, you might try to think like an Arab or a
Chinese or a Scot.

Don't worry so much about "how they would make
it look," but rather "why" it would look that
way. You are really searching for principles
and insights to ideas rather than for actual
details. If you haven't traveled much yourself,
you may wish to take along a seasoned guide--
someone who "speaks the language" of the foreign
place. Ask someone who has done some traveling.

It is easiest to find ideas for "other people's" problems. Everyone likes to pass out "free" advice when someone else seems to have a direction in mind. New ideas are rare. If you do find one you will be all alone, since no one else has ever gone that way.

8 MORPHOLOGICAL FORCED CONNECTIONS

Here is a foolproof idea-invention-finding
scheme.
1. List the attributes of the situation.
2. Below each attribute, place as many alter-
    nates as you can think of. (Use Brain-
    storming.)
3. When completed, make many random runs
    across the lists of alternates, picking
    up a different one from each column and
    assembling the combinations into entirely
    new forms of your original subject.

After all, inventions are merely new ways of
combining old bits and pieces.

EXAMPLE: Subject: Improve a ball-point pen.

Attributes:	FORM	MATERIAL	CAP DETAIL	INK CARTRIDGE
	Cylindrical	Plastic	Separate Cap	Steel Cartridge
	Faceted	Metal	Attached Cap	Plastic Cartridge
	Square	Paper	No Cap	Permanent
	Beaded	Wood	Retracts	Paper Cartridge
	Sculptured	Glass	Cleaning Cap	Cartridge Made of Ink

INVENTION: A Cube Pen; one corner writes leaving
six faces for ads, calendars, photos, etc.

Now you try to invent a new kind of screw driver or
                              sandwich spread
                              drinking fountain
                              blue jeans

9 SEEDS OF IDEAS

To find an idea is to have only one. To find the source of ideas is to have control over their flow.

Don't go looking for ideas directly. Instead, go in search of the seeds of ideas; i.e., the elements from which many ideas can grow.

Many ideas already exist which can be applied, as a principle, to your problem situation.

METHOD:
1. Analyze the principles which you think are involved in your situation.
2. Apply existing ideas for those principles to your situation.

EXAMPLE:
My economics problem involves the principle of reducing wasted motion.

ANSWER:
A toaster heats both sides of the bread simultaneously. How could I do two things at the same time? The refrigerator/sink/stove triangle saves motion in food preparation. How could I rearrange my situation to form a similar work triangle?

Ideas are a dime a dozen. The expense comes about when you begin to develop one of them. Only then does an idea become valuable.

Inventions are but new ways for combining old bits and pieces.

Travel Guides for Ideation

Clark, Charles H., Doubleday
BRAINSTORMING

Osborn, Alex, Scribners
APPLIED IMAGINATION

Parnes, Sidney J., Scribners
CREATIVE BEHAVIOR WORKBOOK and
CREATIVE BEHAVIOR GUIDEBOOK

Parnes, S. J., & Harding, H., Ed., Scribners
A SOURCEBOOK FOR CREATIVE THINKING

_____, Lama Foundation
SEED

Zwicky, Fritz, MacMillan
DISCOVERY, INVENTION, RESEARCH THROUGH THE
  MORPHOLOGICAL APPROACH

Introduction to IDEA-SELECTION

Being conscious of the process you experience increases your creative potential. It is the 'systematic' way: knowing where you are in terms of where you've been and where you intend to be.

Now that you know where it is you want to go (definition) and have devised and collected many alternate ways (ideas) for getting there, the next logical step on the journey will be to select one or more of those "ways" from the many. It is time to decide which idea fulfills the requirements of your objectives better than all of the others...decision-making time.

To be able to choose "the best way," all we need do is to get more and more specific in our description of our definition. The more clearly that your intentions for the behavior of elements of the situation have been stated the easier it will be to find the right means for filling that bill.

It's just that simple. If you get bogged down, you merely clarify the definition a bit more or generate more alternatives and go on again.

Idea-selection is not unlike decision-making of all kinds or types. To do it successfully calls for a firm grasp on your criteria (defined intentions), a clear view of the options available and a strategy or technique for making a connection between the two.

Language Guide for Idea-Selection

A foreign language is simply a different set of symbols for the same reality which confronts us all.

To select ideas is often stated as:

To relate desired outcomes with the various ways for getting there

To make a decision

To find the "best" way to reach the destination

To narrow down our choices

To evaluate "means" by assigning values to "ends"

To determine the way which best satisfies the needs or demands

To compare our goals or intentions with the means for achieving them

To choose one way from all the ways

To decide which action best balances the potential benefits and liabilities of the situation

Etc.

What does selecting ideas mean to you?

Methods for Idea-Selection

1. Screening by Personal Opinion Method
2. Ideas--Objectives Comparison Method
3. The Potpourri Method
4. The Indian Scout Method
5. User-Chooser Method
6. One at a Time Method

1 SCREENING BY PERSONAL OPINION

The most common of all self-determined or self-directed decision-making methods is to judge the options available by passing them through the "screen" or test of personal opinion. It is a technique which calls for stating your personal belief regarding the situation (defining the problem) and comparing possible actions (ideas) with your statement to determine the potential positive or negative consequences of such actions.

Taking a stand is also further evidence of "acceptance" since it includes an inferred agreement to take at least part of the responsibility of any conclusions which might result. It is also a form of self-belief; a willingness to go along with the results of your own analysis. And it expresses faith in your problem-solving abilities...even though new information may emerge at any time causing a possible change of conditions and an accompanying change of your opinion.

To follow this method simply requires you to compare your choices, one against the other, deciding which one or ones best fulfill the statement of definition or intentions...as you have written or stated it. Do this until all apparent options have been so tested or screened. Then choose the one which best fills the bill.

To compare ideas is to uncover the similarities and differences between them. To judge ideas is to relate them to the clearly-defined objectives.

ways to decide from among many options

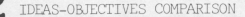

The difference between one idea and another is that one of the two more closely achieves what we intend to happen...problem solving concentrates on making dreams come true.

The more methods we use to evaluate ideas, the more ideal will be the total evaluation.

2 IDEAS-OBJECTIVES COMPARISON

Another basic systematic selection technique is to itemize your goals, objectives and intentions as criteria and to compare those criteria with the alternate means (ideas) for achieving such desired results in a simple matrix. Clearly stated, specific and itemized lists of objectives and alternatives will produce the most easily managed matrix. By such comparison, you methodically discard those ideas which do not work as well as others until only those which are generally satisfactory remain.

In the matrix, list your objectives on one axis and your ideas on the other. Scoring can be simplified by writing YES at intersections where individual ideas and criteria agree and NO where they do not. MAYBE or (?) could be used when an uncertainty exists (suggesting more study). Complex situations may require a more specific numerical evaluation.

CATEGORIZATION OF IDEAS is a helpful preselection operation. If all ideas are organized into more manageable groups of similar kinds of things, a great number of ideas can be evaluated quickly. This is a generally useful method which can be adapted in intensity to any problem situation.

3 POTPOURRI

A typical sub-problem accompanying the decision-making phase is the pain of leaving the others behind as one alternative is chosen as best. Two variations exist which make it possible to have your cake and eat it too. The first strategy is to expand each alternative into two or more additional alternatives so that their familiarity is lessened. Then when a selection is made it seems as though no one was "preferred" and the others "slighted." A more typical method is to combine the good points of all your alternatives into one large response, thus leaving none behind and benefitting from them all.

EXAMPLE: If ideas 1, 2 and 3 are:
        1. to take a vacation
        2. to continue working
        3. to find a vacation substitute
A POTPOURRI which combines all three might be:
        4. to turn work into a vacation;
A scheme which utilizes the essential concepts
of all (3) three original ideas.

4 THE INDIAN SCOUT

The most commonly practiced technique for
selecting ideas is to try them out ahead of
time via the use of some simulation device.
Like the Indian scouts of the last century,
you go up ahead to see what it's going to
be like when the main force arrives. You check
things out to improve your chances of avoiding
an ambush or other disaster. This method is
based on the premise that if you use your
imagination (or other form of simulated reality)
to experience each of your ideas, you will be
in a better position to choose from among
them. The Indian Scout technique attempts to
answer the question, "What could possibly happen
if you actually carried this idea to completion?"

The Program Evaluation Review Technique (P.E.R.T.)
provides an organized procedure for exploring
this method in depth. With P.E.R.T., you
attempt to determine "the most critical path"
in order to avoid being victimized by your
ignorance of its importance later on. For
more on this method refer to TRAVEL GUIDES
for idea-selecting on the next page.

Remember to ask yourself how you "feel" about the ideas you evaluate. You may discover that a seemingly best idea really gives you emotional "fits" and won't be comfortable at all.

Unclear objectives make it impossible to decide between the alternative ways of proceeding to a goal.

5 USER-CHOOSER

At times certain problem-situations warrant
the inclusion of outside assistance in the
decision-making phase...times when your decision
alone would be overly manipulative of others
or where your lack of experience somewhat
disqualifies you from taking total command.

To simplify matters it would be helpful if
you would organize the existing points-of-view
(defined criteria) as well as the options being
considered in such a way as to eliminate confusion
and facilitate choice for those who may not
have been consciously involved with the situation
as you have been. Take caution not to "stack
the deck" in your favor or the method is de-
feated before completion.

6 ONE AT A TIME

The inability to decide quite often leads to trying this final time-worn method...taking the options in a "one by one" experimental sequence until all of them have been given a trial. Apparently the long, hard, painful way to choose, this method can nonetheless work when others fail or seem inappropriate. Again, sorting and categorizing the options may save unnecessary repetition or inconsistent treatment of the alternatives.

Enjoying your freedom of choice can be lots of work in that dealing systematically with choosing between lots of ideas often forces us to spend a great deal of time clarifying objectives.

Travel Guides for Idea-Selection

Churchman, C., Delta
THE SYSTEMS APPROACH

Churchman, C., et al, Wiley
INTRODUCTION TO OPERATIONS RESEARCH

Cook, Desmond, U.S. Office of Educ.
P.E.R.T. (PROGRAM EVALUATION REVIEW TECHNIQUE)
"THE CRITICAL PATH METHOD"

Evarts, Harry F., Allyn & Bacon
INTRODUCTION TO PERT

Osgood, Suci, Tannenbaum, Univ. of Ill.
THE MEASUREMENT OF MEANING

Parnes, Sidney J., Scribners
CREATIVE BEHAVIOR WORKBOOK

Sanoff, Henry, School of Design, N.C.
  State Univ.
TECHNIQUES OF EVALUATION FOR DESIGNERS

Introduction to IMPLEMENTATION

Implementation is that segment of the problem-solving process where the idea chosen (in the previous stage) as the one best able to satisfy your intentions is at last put to a test. Implementing your choice is the "moment of truth"...planning for the most part is over. The foundations for taking considered and determined action have been completed. You are ready to actively improve the problem posed in its original situational terms. You are prepared to test your involvement and skills at analysis, definition, idea generation and decision-making. Implementation is the pay-off.

You should now be prepared to enter the tactical, active state of translating your carefully selected alternative (idea) into the reality of a solution. There should be excitement in the pleasurable experience of knowing where you are going and why: while enjoying the security of having explored many alternate concepts and routes along the way.

Travelers who have followed a systematic sequence as outlined in this guidebook are hopefully no longer the awkward problem-solving tourists who would act on impulse alone. Instead, by applying the logic of the design process, they should now be more balanced, integrated and holistic, well-seasoned travelers.

Implementation can begin by simply picking up the phone and ordering a round trip ticket to your destination. It means "get going." You are ready for action. The time has come for you to put your chosen idea(s) to work.

Language Guide for Implementation

Words are symbolic sounds which stand for meanings which stand for reality as it was perceived by the speaker. They are far from reality but they are the best means we have for objectifying our subjective experiences.

To implement a selected idea is often stated as:

*putting the plan into effect
*taking action on the chosen idea
*giving embodiment to the concept
*giving form to the idea
*optimizing the intentions
*achieving the solution
*doing it, getting it on, getting on with it
*putting it together
*synthesizing
*realizing or actualizing the solution
*achieving the concrete, real, final product

Depending on what you do or need to do, implementation may take the form of one or more of these activities:

acting**arguing**accepting**administering

baking**balancing**bicycling**blocking

breaking**building**buying**canvassing

cleaning**composing**cooking**detailing

digging**drawing**driving**eating

enjoying**facilitating**finding**flying

grinding**helping**inventing**jazzing

jumping**kidding**learning**lecturing

listing**milling**mourning**nesting

nibbling**owning**painting**planning**playing

quieting**raking**reporting**running

sculpting**seeing**selling**spending**teaching

telling**testing**traveling**using**wishing, etc.

Which actions must you now take in order to implement your chosen idea?

Methods for Implementation

1. The Brainwashing Method
2. The Time-Task Schedule Technique
3. The Performance Specifications Method
4. The Advocacy Method
5. The Attribute Analog, or "You can build a computer at home in your spare time" Method
6. "Live up to your name" Technique
7. THE NATIVE ARTISANS' FLEA MARKET
    A. Principles of Design Method
    B. Diagrams and Schematics Method
    C. Models Approach
    D. Bionics Method
    E. Follow a Similar Model Method
    F. Pattern Language
    G. Archetypical Form Method
    H. Common Denominator Method
    I. Essential Unit Building Block Technique
    J. Holistic Method
    K. Response to Human Needs Method
    L. "Let George do it" Technique
    M. Consultants Team Technique
    N. Structural Limits Method
    O. The "Topsy" Technique
    P. Response to Role-Playing Method
    Q. Notation Systems Technique
    R. Inspiration or Lightning Bolt Approach
    S. Trial and Error Method

(What other methods can you suggest?)

1 THE TIME-TASK SCHEDULE

A basic way to get on with the tactical phase of your problem excursion is to make a time-task schedule. The procedure for this is:

1. Decide how many and what kind of tasks are involved in performing the selected idea requirements. Answer the question, "What are all the steps which must be taken in order to complete this thing?" Be picky about identifying even small tasks since it is those little things which eventually add up to the total job.

Plan to have an occasional "rest stop" to recharge and to examine how well things are going.

82

Plan ahead. Before diving right in to following one idea, try to imagine what it would be like if the trip were already over. The consequences of following a wrong idea could be worse than following no idea at all.

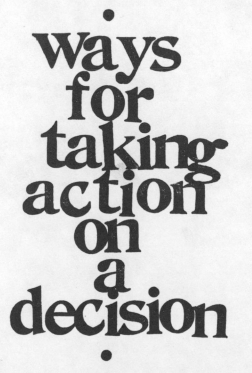

Since actions speak louder than words, try not to scream with your feet in your mouth.

2. Carefully determine the amount of time available for the overall project. Don't kid yourself.

3. Assign, in the most reasonable way you can, portions of the total time to each of the small tasks found in Step 1.

4. Prepare a graph which shows the relationship of your time to your tasks.

5. Allow the time-task graph to guide you through the implementation phase.

2 BRAINWASHING

Taking action on an idea is not very much different from accepting the responsibility for solving the problem at the outset. The main difference is that in the beginning what lies ahead is unknown. By now you have gone through five (5) phases of a systematic excursion, and should be confident. But, physical and emotional strength is probably still required for "getting it on." You may even have to go back to some of the self-motivation methods from the initial phase of the process and brainwash all misgivings and fears from your head to find the courage to go on. You may have to reconvince yourself of the logic of your process and any personal reasons you may have had at the outset.

Note: BRAINWASHING is a pre-implementation method and is useful in combination with all other implementation methods.

ways for taking action on a decision

3 PERFORMANCE SPECIFICATION

Intentions can be changed into action by breaking them down into small specific behaviors. Once the exact bit by bit performance you desire is specified, all that remains is to translate it into real actions, materials or other physical forms.

In essence, this is a technique for a continual elaboration on the selected idea until it stops being abstract and starts being concrete or real. The more that each specific aspect of the idea can be stated in terms of performance, the closer that idea comes to being realized (turned into reality).

EXAMPLE:

If your implementation requirement had been
to move out of your dull room and find a
livlier, friendlier place to live, the
SPECIFICATIONS FOR PERFORMANCE might begin
to read like this--

Find an apartment where other people
having interests similar to mine live.

Look for a place which has a recreational
history of parties and social exchange.

Swimming pools, saunas, game rooms and
nearby shopping are a must.

Etc.

Note! If the exact specification of performances
begins to look like a list of exactly specified
"objectives," it is because they are synonymous.

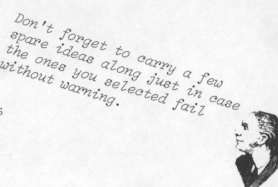

Don't forget to carry a few
spare ideas along just in case
the ones you selected fail
without warning.

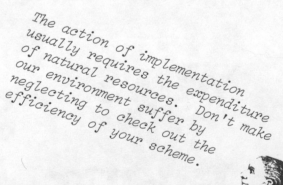

The action of implementation
usually requires the expenditure
of natural resources. Don't make
our environment suffer by
neglecting to check out the
efficiency of your scheme.

4 ADVOCACY

Another way to get an idea going is to help it
to help itself. For instance, try to explain
to the beneficiaries of the idea how they can
pull it forward while you get behind and push.
An architect might help clients become amateur
environmental designers and thereby receive
"inside help" in achieving their mutual goals.
If the idea selected for implementation was
something impersonal, such as "to inaugurate
one day a week when no cigarettes will be
smoked," it can be encouraged to help itself
by supporting it with additional bolstering
ideas. In this particular case, the supportive
ideas might include: Replace cigarettes with
a substitute need; make a reward and a penalty
for achievers and non-achievers, set up a
mock trial for those caught smoking, etc.

5 ATTRIBUTE ANALOG or YOU CAN BUILD A COMPUTER AT HOME IN YOUR SPARE TIME

Slide rules are really analog computers. With them, two sets of scales may be related to each other. The relationships may be varied within established limits to reveal resultant values. A centigrade-Fahrenheit thermometer does the same thing using mercury as one scale for sliding up and down a numerical scale. And so do certain children's construction kits which contain programmed interchangeable parts able to be assembled into many variations of the same things if prescribed (scaled) operations are followed.

If your idea has definitely fixed limits and yet could take a wide variety of forms, you may wish to build an analog computer to use as a tool for studying many possible combinations which could be achieved within those limits.

Similar to the morphological methods, your "computer" might allow any combination of potentials to be assembled as long as those combinations stayed within the prescribed limits of the selected idea. Your computer might be linear or circular. It could take many shapes, forms and variations. Your hand or pencil might be the only moving part.

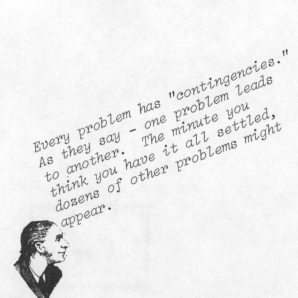

6 LIVE UP TO YOUR NAME

Names help us to identify the various people, things, places and events of our experience. Once named, a formerly complex assortment of bits and pieces comes together in our minds as a totality. Similarly, it is possible to begin an active translation of an idea into physical form by finding a name for that idea which seems to pull its parts together as a whole and to then give form to the name.

EXAMPLE:

Suppose your idea was to triple the enrollment of the local Eco-Action group by throwing a recycling party. Give the party a name: Let's say you call it "Smashing Good Time." What remains is to live up to that name. Have the band call themselves the "Can Smashers." Invent a dance called the "Carton Twister." Print 'invites' on can bottoms and tops. Have a can-smashing competition and a bottle-breaking race, etc. It's easy. Once you've got a title, what remains is merely to fill in the blanks.

7 Flea Market

Here are twenty (20) additional implementation
methods. They are merely some of the ways that
problem solvers in the arts use to express
their ideas. Although these methods have been
gleaned mostly from the visual design disciplines,
it is not unlikely to find them being used by
other artful and scientific designers (creative
problem solvers) in general. Whether Art or
Science, a problem remains a problem within any
discipline. Its truths must still be uncovered
(scientific activity) and those truths must be
communicated (artistic activity). The methods
given are adaptable to many diverse problem
conditions.

A) PRINCIPLES OF DESIGN

Implementing ideas is often defined as
composing or synthesizing wholes from
parts. Many diverse and personal composi-
tional rules and principles exist for
putting things together, but one set which
seems universally common to them all are
these:
HARMONY or Recognizable similarity for all
   parts of the whole
CONTRAST or Recognizable difference for
   all parts of the whole
BALANCE or Recognizable stability for all
   parts of the whole
ORDER or Recognizable pattern of organization
   to the whole
UNITY or Recognizable collectiveness for
   all parts of the whole
The fact that the Principles of Design are easily
translated from and attributed to the natural
laws of physical behavior attests to their
universal validity.

B) DIAGRAMS AND SCHEMATICS

Designers often begin the implementation
phase with scribbled diagrams and schematics
to symbolize relationships between the parts
of problems. They search, via sketchy
organizational diagrams and lists, for the
relationships which link the factors and
aspects or components of their problem.
We hear such diagrams called "bubble"
diagrams, "flow" charts, layouts, organizational charts, etc. Through repetition,
and by trial and error, the sketches eventually emerge as refined definitive relationship drawings which are then translated
into physical materials.

C) MODELS

Although we realize that because of endless interrelationships just about anything can be used as a model for the study of another thing, some problem situations just seem to call for constructing small "scale" models as a method for moving from the abstract to the real. Complex forms and difficult-to-visualize ideas often demand to be "mocked up" in order for "parts" to be visualized in context with "wholes." The normal procedure is to begin with rough "study" or "sketch" models and to work through a series of models until a "finished model" or "working prototype" is developed.

D) BIONICS

Bionics, the science of interrelating natural and man-made systems, is still another variation on the MODELS approach. The basic difference is that the bionic model is a natural one. For every possible idea some natural counterpart can be found. By studying how the natural model works and how it survives or achieves its ends, the implementation of your idea will find its guidelines.

Being a part of nature and also being able to (mentally) stand apart from nature it is possible to allow nature to model the behavior of your human intentions.

E) FOLLOWING A SIMILAR MODEL

Finding a problem similar to yours which has been solved to the satisfaction of all concerned is another common technique. You might review how someone else implemented their problem and assemble yours in the same way.

This approach, though often misnamed "cribbing," is really a form of apprenticeship. When used consciously we can express a wish to learn by following a leader and are perhaps wise enough to realize how foolish it would be to overtly avoid the experience of others.

F) PATTERN LANGUAGE

A variation on the similar model technique is pattern language. Within every problem situation many sub-problems exist. For each of those sub-problems, socially, psychologically and physically-acceptable solutions already exist. If a large number of these sub-problems within a system can

87

be identified and if acceptable solutions
to each of them can be logically recalled,
a language of the behavioral "patterns" of
the problem situation begins to emerge.
The PATTERN LANGUAGE method suggests using
that context of sub-solutions as a language
to derive new systems. (This regenerative
technique is still in development by a group
in Berkeley under the direction of C. J.
Alexander.)

G) ARCHETYPICAL-STEREOTYPICAL FORM

Typical repeated internal and external
forces and pressures acting on a situation
tend to give things archetypical forms which
reflect response to such forces. Change
being normally an evolutionary process, we
eventually learn the archetypes of our
environment and respond with them rather
than with ever new solutions. A child
draws a gable roof and bearing walls to
represent a house. And such a drawing
represents the stereotype of house, while
the triangular "trussed" roof shape also
reflects the structural archetype for that
situation.

This design technique approaches the synthesis of new things by casting them within
the mold of the archetype. Books are flat
and rectangular, churches point to the sky,
cups are tapered cylinders, etc.

Archetypes and stereotypes can be thought
of as the traditional or original prototypes
of things.

H) COMMON DENOMINATOR

Complex or multi-part ideas may be more
easily implemented by locating a common
denominator--an element, unit or component
which gives every part of the intended idea
some common relationship. For example, use
of a grid to compare interrelations of
idea attributes might yield one or more of
them as being influential over all the
others. By responding to such a common
relationship a designer can ease the task
of implementation, because common denomina-
tors tend to be independent variables; they
can be used as a framework for managing the
remainder of the systems we construct.

I) ESSENTIAL UNIT BUILDING BLOCK

A House of Cards and a "castle" made from
children's building blocks are examples of
larger things achieved by assembling small
typical or identical units and by following

a consistent set of "rules" or limits for
assembly. In a similar way, other large
or apparently complex systems can be con-
structed. This method begins with a search
for an essential unit which can later be
assembled in quantity to achieve large and
complex "configurations" not easily possible
when all parts are allowed to be individually
unique. "Small units" grow into larger
systems by following determined consistent
rules of interconnection and assembly. The
Essential Unit Building Block Method can
be seen to be a variation of the Common
Denominator Method. Still another name
for this technique is UNIT GROWTH.

J) HOLISTIC OR TOTAL FORM

The Unit Growth approach begins with small
units and assembles them into larger wholes.
The opposite approach, often referred to as
the Sculptural, Holistic or Total Form
Method, begins with whole assemblages con-
ceived as abstract configurations and proceeds to break those wholes down into orderly
systems of smaller components. It should
be clear that no matter which of the two
(UNIT GROWTH OR HOLISTIC) methods is chosen,
it is not long before the other must also
be considered. Only a few small units
may be assembled before it becomes necessary
to consider the total form which might emerge.
Similarly, attempts to generate whole forms
can be taken only so far before attention
must be given to the components needed to
realize those totalities.

K) RESPONSE TO HUMAN NEEDS

This method contends that all problems in
some way begin as unsatisfied need and
that solutions must be acceptable responses
to the human needs which inspired them in
the first place. Lists of human needs are
still somewhat rare, but researchers are
fast collecting them. In the interim, lists
which are available suffice to help produce
solutions having far more humanistic concerns than before. They include the full
range of physical (survival) needs such
as food, rest, shelter, etc., as well as
the many psychological needs such as self-
respect, friendship, achievement and order-
liness. Ideas being implemented are
checked against "needs" on the list and
implemented as a response to them. Since
human individuality is an expression of the
separate, unique proportions we each have
of a common set of needs, you can be sure
that implementation based on this technique
will never satisfy all persons involved.

89

To use this method, the essence or core of
the idea is first reviewed and translated
into "needs" terminology. The new statement
is then used as the ultimate decision-making
screen for all further decisions in the
implementation phase. Such an approach
simulates the entire problem-solving process.
It distills a definition (essence) from a
previously defined situation and proceeds
to use that new definition as a primary
source for evaluating all other decisions
pertaining to the situation.

L) LET GEORGE DO IT

A popular method for entirely circumventing
any possible trauma involved with personal
implementation of an idea is to get a
"patent" on the thing and sell it to someone
else in a better position to act on it than
you are. Simply, "draw it up" (which in
itself might take a bit of "working out"
to accomplish), hire a patent attorney to
authorize a patent search, wait for the
results and if approved go out looking
for a developer willing to buy your scheme.
A still simpler variation is to talk someone
into doing the entire thing for you.

M) CONSULTANTS TEAM

Become a team leader. Break your idea down
into the various categories which can be
individually acted out by experts. If, for
instance, your idea deals with the development
of a new product, divide it into the separate
areas of market analysis, design, production,
advertising, distribution, etc. Arrange to
meet the various consultant teams who know
each of those areas best. You act as the
coordinator who resolves all of the opinions
of your "expert" staff. The theory here is
that the more people you get in on the act,
the better will be the total performance.
The dangers are either that the performance
will have so many prima donnas it will be
difficult to recognize the idea beneath it
or that the idea will lose sight of its
objectives due to one of the experts being
stronger than the coordinator.

N) STRUCTURAL LIMITS METHOD

Every assemblage has a structural framework
which holds it together and stabilizes its
form. This is true for music and dance
notations just as it is for buildings and
bridges, and all structures have limits
which, if exceeded, cause failure or collapse
of the system. To operate by the STRUCTURAL

LIMITS METHOD is simply to allow the "structure" or system of loads, stresses and
reactions to stress for purposes of main-
taining stability to be a limiting factor.
In the end there will be a cohesiveness or
equilibrium about the whole which is undeniable.
Although this method is common to problems of
civil engineering it is nonetheless adaptable
to other problems.

O) TOPSY

It's not uncommon to find a designer operating
without an "M.O." (modus operandus, or
method of operation) except that it might
be called TOPSY...by simply letting it
happen," "letting nature take its course"
or "working it on out." This non-directed
approach of course has shortcomings, such as
difficulties with time limits, not knowing
what to do next, wasted energy, etc. Still,
with persistence, this method can be made
to work.

Because guidelines are uncovered by bits and
pieces during the process, the TOPSY approach
is like operating in the dark: a situation
which can cause loss of confidence.

P) RESPONSE TO ROLE-PLAYING

If you want personal experience with implementation, you may have to get into the act. This
is a technique of becoming the thing, playing
the role of the people affected by your
ideas. It is an expression of the imagination
and therefore requires image-making skills.
As a method, Role-playing is a technique of
living through the experience of implementation before it actually happens and later
responding to that experience in a more
informed way. The pre-experience allows
fears to be acted out and eliminated and
can provide the security of "having been
there before."

Q) NOTATION SYSTEMS

When your job requires you to implement great
numbers of similar complex problems, it may
be advantageous to develop your own notation
system. Numbers and words and other symbols
are devised to simplify the apparently complex problem of dealing with reality.

You might develop a personal notation system
to help you visualize or deal with large
quantities of information simultaneously.
It can save needless repetition of operations
during developmental processes, and it can

insure the inclusion of necessary considerations which might otherwise be inadvertently ignored. Take a look at musical or mathematical notation for inspiration; remembering that a few symbols can greatly simplify many repetitive processes.

R) INSPIRATION OR LIGHTNING BOLT

Lots of problem solvers use the age-old technique of just waiting around for inspiration. They read, talk, scribble and wait. They know about their problem and now expect the lightning bolt of inspiration to hit them in the back of the neck. When it hits, they shout something like "Eureka" and then get on with it. This method is often used for "definition" and "ideation" as well as implementation. Alex Osborn calls it "incubation." Its general symbol is a light bulb shining over the head of the enlightened problem solver. This approach is probably the most untrustworthy of the lot since it is highly dependent on factors outside of your control, which misleads many to believe in magic, fate and design-by-luck as substitutes for goal achievement by intention and orderly process.

When you're headed toward a goal of your own, it is not unusual to cross paths with others going to different places.

S) TRIAL AND ERROR

Evolution and the Law of Natural Selection both express this well-known technique for developing ideas into reality through stages of trial and error. This is a strategy of implementing and evaluating over and over with a view to eliminating error from your actions. No matter how sophisticated methods become, the TRIAL and ERROR method will continue to exist. Because when you are totally finished with the implementation and evaluation of any problem-solving journey you must invariably say, "The next time I <u>try</u> this kind of thing, I certainly won't make the <u>errors</u> that were made this time.

Travel Guide for Implementation

Hiscox, Gardner, ed., Books, Inc.
HENLEY'S TWENTIETH CENTURY BOOK OF FORMULAS,
  PROCESSES AND TRADE SECRETS

McKim, Robert H., Brooks/Cole
EXPERIENCES IN VISUAL THINKING

Maslow, Abraham, Van Nostrand
TOWARD A PSYCHOLOGY OF BEING

McHarg, Ian, Nat'l History Press
DESIGN WITH NATURE

Perin, Constance, MIT
WITH MAN IN MIND

Polya, G., Doubleday
HOW TO SOLVE IT

Introduction to EVALUATION

One final Energy State remains--Evaluation--the time taken both during and at the end of the problem-solving journey for review. We look back to determine how far we have traveled and how valuable the journey has been so that the remainder of our trip and future trips will be more smooth.

Evaluation is a time for accounting; for comparing actions with consequences; for detecting flaws and making improvements; for planting the seeds of future challenge. Since it requires getting both inside and outside of self to see ourselves more clearly, it can become an anxious time of being "off center."

To evaluate is to measure how far or how much (quantity) and how well or how rich (quality). The sum of the two represents the total "value" or what a journey is worth. And it cannot be accomplished without having laid the proper foundation of objectives; i.e., realistic measurement of how far we have traveled or how rich the trip has been is improbable if we didn't clearly state where it was that we intended to go in the first place.

After a trip or two, it becomes clear that creative problem-solving journeys can be digested to the simple process of defining, achieving and measuring objectives; that the process of design is really just a systematic series of events which leads us to determine how far and/or how well we can make our dreams come true.

Evaluations are not conclusions; they are commencements. They end one journey and carry us on to the more knowledgeable beginning of another journey. Just as commencement means both to complete and to begin, so evaluation is a link between our problem-solving journeys.

94

Language Guide for Evaluation

Descriptive as they may seem, most words are still at least two steps removed from reality.

Be sure to list all extra-curricular contingencies as you prepare to evaluate your process. It is easy to miss the specific value of the bits of experience when your attention is glued to goal attainment alone.

Evaluating the problem-solving process is often stated as:

*looking back to determine the quantity and quality of our achievement
*examining changes in behavior over time
*getting outside of ourselves for a more objective view
*taking a critical look at our process
*self-criticizing
*reviewing our actions in order to better determine how to proceed
*talking it over; appraising what we have done
*editing the report of our experiences
*describing a newly developed view of a problem situation
*assigning value or worth to achievement
*turning experience into something measurable
*reflecting on the journey
*presenting the travelogue of a journey

What does "to evaluate the process" mean to you?

Methods for Evaluation

1. Measuring Progress Method
2. "Who Else Has an Opinion?" Method
3. Progress Chart Method
4. Letter to Your Best Friend Method
5. Academic Method

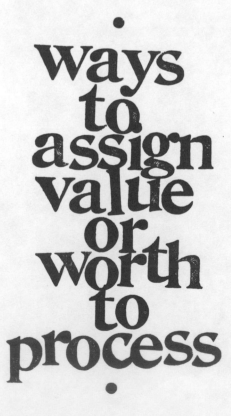

1 MEASURING PROGRESS (ACCORDING TO PERSONAL OPINION)

In a most systematic view, an evaluation is a comparison of objectives with results. It initially asks, "What did you hope for and plan to happen?" and then measures those dreams against what actually did happen. From the measurement the problem solver can discover the quantity and quality of progress.

EXAMPLE: GUIDE TO EVALUATION

A. Statement of Goals
B. Objectives Described in Measurable Terms
C. Achievement
   1. How far did I go? (quantitative; amount)
       Number of objectives reached
   2. How well did I do? (qualitative; enrich-
      ment)
      Benefits accrued
        Educational: Knowledge acquired
                 Skills developed
                 Attitudes altered
                    or reinforced
D. Contingencies
   1. Unforeseen benefits outside of objectives
   2. Unforeseen problems outside of my intention
   3. Additional objectives discovered late
      in the process
   4. Change of intention during process
      which nullifies initial objectives
E. Comparison of Goals with Achievement
   1. Point by point comparison and rating
   2. Scale of standards description
   3. Review and reinforcement of behavior
      changes
F. Plans for the Future

. ways to assign value or worth to process .

2 "WHO ELSE HAS AN OPINION?"

At first glance, the writing of a questionnaire seems easy. But you can be sure that the preparation of "a survey of user needs or public opinion which collects measurable results" requires experience, skill and strict attention. Most questionnaires achieve little in terms of evaluative results. They merely pacify those who prepare them with "general feelings" that things went either right or wrong or somewhere in between and offer little help for improvement.

The key to preparing an evaluative questionnaire is identical to that for preparing a set of measurable objectives: The answers obtained must be received in a form which is relative to intentional improvement. Here are some definite methods for preparing such a survey or questionnaire.

TRY NOT TO ASK GENERAL QUESTIONS
  You'll only get general or stereotyped answers which will lose importance in their translation.

WATCH YOUR LANGUAGE
  Don't ask "foreigners" to use your language or expect them to understand your special jargon the way you do.

TRY TO GET ANSWERS TRANSLATED INTO MORE THAN ONE FORM
  Ask for words, pictures, numbers, behavior, etc., to get a more complete response.

NARROW DOWN
  Work from the general to the specific so an order is clearly established

WHEN IN ROME
  Pose your questions in a form familiar to them...not you. Remember that what seems friendly to you may still be strange to others. Relaxation and openness is difficult in a strange situation.

DON'T BE A SELF-FULFILLING PROPHET
  Don't beg for answers which support your opinion. Such an approach makes the questionnaire meaningless.

GIVE A REWARD
  Make it worthwhile to answer your questions. After all, you are taking their answers to keep for yourself.

BE DIRECT
  Try not to be vague or poetic. Answers which came in that form would be difficult to translate.

PROGRESS CHART

If you have tried making a chart relating your
defined objectives (tasks) with your available
time, you have already found a simple way to keep
a running evaluation. When you keep the chart up
to date it allows you to see, at a glance, how far
along you are in terms of meeting your objectives.
This method usually works best for quantitative
measures but quality can be added in the form of
side notes or comments made in a journal of progress
or personal improvement.

4 LETTER TO YOUR BEST FRIEND METHOD

Another painless way to determine the value of
your excursions through intentional achievement
is to write a letter about them. Simply write
as if to a friend or parent (you could easily
play the role of your own best friend). Describe your accomplishments and what they mean
to you in terms of your initial intentions and
how they developed along the way. Tell how
valuable they are in both a broad sense and
specific sense. You might even mail it for
still more feedback...or mail it to yourself
to see how it sounds several days from now.

 ACADEMIC METHOD

If you are looking for common ground between
students, teachers and school administrators, you
will be sure to find it surrounding the subject
of grades and grading...few, if any, appreciate
the potential or intrinsic educational value
of its process. Grades are usually referred
to as being the sickness of academia. Yet if
considered as an evaluative strategy, with
intentions for revealing suggestions regarding
behavioral change, the process of grading can
be far more meaningful than the symbolic letter
or number which appears so irrelevant to so many.

When classroom and coursework objectives are
mutually derived and clearly expressed in
measurable terms, incremental evaluations produce
understandable and improvement-oriented grades
throughout the entire period of study. The
ultimate symbolic A's, B's, C's, etc., once
more gain meaning as they are found to be
useful shorthand notations for evaluative
thinking in a continuous and not merely
after-the-fact sense.

Try "grading" your own problem-solving journey
and the need for criteria in the form of clearly
measurable objectives will soon emerge as
important.

*Prejudice is a poor companion
to take along to an evaluation
session.*

*In academic evaluations, the
letter grade (A, B, C, D, F,
etc.) which stands for a word
description (Superior, Better
than Average, Average, Barely
Passing, etc. becomes an abstract
symbolic way of measuring how
well the stated course objectives were met. In that true
sense, they are a clever code--
a shorthand system for a multi-
faceted measurement.*

Travel Guides for Evaluation

Churchman, C. W., Wiley
MEASUREMENT: DEFINITIONS AND THEORIES

Leopold, Luna B., et al, U.S. Dept. of Interior
A PROCEDURE FOR EVALUATING ENVIRONMENTAL
   IMPACT, Geol. Survey Circular 645

Mager, Robert, Fearon
GOAL ANALYSIS

Mager, Robert, Fearon
PREPARING INSTRUCTIONAL OBJECTIVES

Rokeach, Milton, The Free Press
THE NATURE OF HUMAN VALUES

Question! What does an evaluation of a trip usually reveal?

Answer: Measures of achievement, need for improvement plus the fact ...

...that the process never ends...

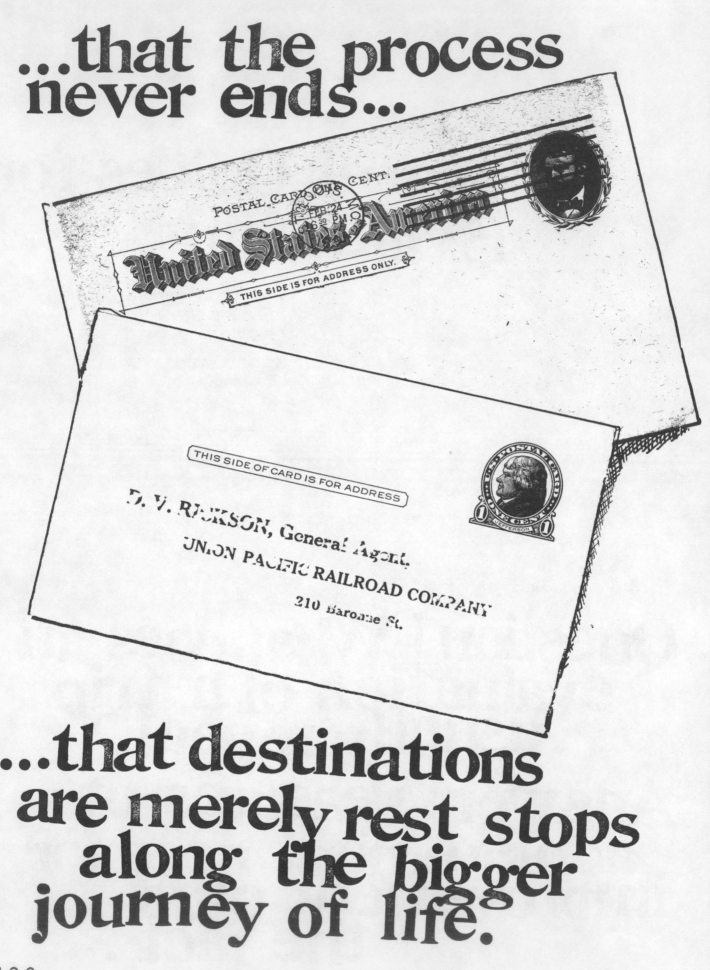

POSTAL CARD ONE CENT.

FEB 24
6 30 PM

United States of America

THIS SIDE IS FOR ADDRESS ONLY.

THIS SIDE OF CARD IS FOR ADDRESS

D. V. RICKSON, General Agent.
UNION PACIFIC RAILROAD COMPANY
210 Baronne St.

U.S. POSTAL CARD
ONE CENT
JEFFERSON

...that destinations are merely rest stops along the bigger journey of life.

Back home with the memorabilia

Looking back over a completed journey is a
mellowing experience. The good times and bad
tend to fuse together to become a single memory
or general impression. Such general impressions
are merely accented by those most memorable
experiences encountered; minor pleasures and
acquisitions are as easily forgotten as are
some minor difficulties and sub-problems. As
we lose sight of the small experiences and
begin to remember only the major "ports of
call," we set ourselves up once again to forget
the joy and reality of process orientation.
We recall our total, multi-event experience as
but a series of products or destinations.

Thinking this way makes improvement difficult
since the task of determining value can become a search for only the superficial. By
viewing our process of interwoven and diverse
activities as necessary and important trivia
occurring between goals we can make a continual
survey of benefits accrued and losses suffered
as we proceed.

Learning from our experiences requires us to
concentrate on their interrelationships. If
we wish to improve skills or develop knowledge
and values, we must work toward improving the
bits and pieces (objectives) of the process
(goal). Conscious travel through the seven
ENERGY STATES of the overall process makes the
gathering and organizing of "notes" and memora-
bilia easier. With such materials to review,
the potential for learning from our journey
is improved. We can begin to concentrate on
and thus appreciate the many events which occur
along the way. With such a consciousness,
the improvements and behavioral changes which
comprise a learning condition exist.

We will all derive separate and unique values
from our experiences. And we will then go on
to judge future experiences against those
personal values, modifying and formulating
new values in the process. We call the complete
process 'learning'; the chief by-product of
life.

During the course of presenting the seven Energy
States and the many methods of the problem-
solving process, our intention has been to help
you realize a creative necessity for locating a
personally-tailored balance between the need to
set and realize goals and the need to enjoy
life as it unfolds. To appreciate the entirety
of life, we believe it is necessary to develop
skill in walking the fence between process-
awareness and goals-achievement. And we hope
your personal discovery of this fundamental
requirement has been enjoyable.

To help remind yourself of the benefit accrued
from this balanced condition, you might try
imagining the difference in time between
arrivals at various stations on a railway
schedule or between stops on a bus line. It
takes time, often lots of it, to reach the
various objectives along the journey to our
goals. The moments of achievement approach,
arrive and pass and we are off once more to
the next destination. In the end, it is
clear that we have spent the vast portion of
our life in the process of going and only a
very small part of it in arriving.

SIDE TRIPS

Separating the TRAVELERS from the tourists

Why Side Trips ?

It is the difference in quantity and quality of the side trips which separate the tourists from the well-seasoned travelers in the world of problem solving. The more extra-curricular discoveries encountered along the way, the more interesting and meaningful will be the travelog in the end.

Of course, side trips can also become delay or avoidance tactics and act as tourist traps just as they can become mind-expanding experiences. In this section, we offer a selection of side trips for beginning problem solvers. We hope they will enrich your trip through this book.

CREATIVITY GAMES

What most people refer to as creative behavior is those actions which seem to apply an unusual technique in a conscious or subconscious way. Breaking rules or habits without an undue amount of stress is typical of such behavior. But creative behavior could be more truly defined as behavior which is both subjectively and objectively whole, free from pride and other "deadly sins," expressive of constructive discontent and a willingness to succeed <u>and</u> is fearless in the face of rules or habits.

Since any change in behavior denotes the breaking of a habit, any game which produces change is a habit-breaking exercise. Here are a series of games designed to help with the learning and development of those "traits."

Games to develop Belief in Self

Write a column for your local paper describing how well you have solved some important problem. Tell about how you were able to achieve what you did. Be as laudatory as possible. Describe in detail what a really good person you were (are).

1

2 Design a monument to your dreams. What form will it take? Why? Where will it be located? Why? How long should it last? Why?

3 Explain to some friends how difficult it is to do what you do but how well you accept your responsibility for doing it despite those difficulties. Brag just a little.

4 Imagine that you have just won the Nobel Prize for humanity which brings fame and fortune your way. Now that you are well known and economically secure and no longer need be concerned with those gnawing distractions, imagine how well you can achieve other current goals.

5 Try to go a whole week without explaining or excusing yourself to anyone. Forget apologies and other humbling practices for this week. Be a little pushy. Ask for favors you wouldn't normally ask others to perform. This game is an exercise in releasing yourself from the imagined controls of others.

Games to develop

Freedom from Pride

1 Pride often leads us to behave contrary to our feelings. Try to decide how you actually feel about some matter of importance and allow that feeling to rule your behavior in every situation and contact. Don't behave one way in front of your friend and another in front of your boss and still another in front of your parents. Stay with your feeling and express it consistently.

2 Get someone to take a movie of you doing some everyday thing like having a conversation. Make sure that you get long shots, medium shots and close-ups and that you see yourself from front, side, rear, below and above. This is one sure way to discover how different you actually are from what you may proudly imagine.

For about 15 minutes each day try to behave and think like the person you dislike most. Try it for a few days to see if it is easier to deal with your pride when next near that person.

3

Break some fear habits:

4

a) Don't answer the phone the next 5 times it rings and examine why the phone has such power over your attention.

b) The next time someone says something which sounds or seems outrageous to you (something bigoted, insulting or fallacious), put it straight by speaking out. Try not to be aggressive or chicken-hearted. Simply state your objection as calmly as possible. A rehearsal might help iron out excuses or unnecessary digs brought on by your anger.

c) Don't allow your pride/fear to waste your time. The next boring lecture you attend can be made less boring if you ask lots of questions and make an attempt to get the subject matter into a personally relevant form.

Games to develop

Constructive Discontent

Try to see what a problem feels like from someone else's point-of-view...Close your eyes and form images of what seems to be implied by the following statements:

1

a) The president of a college addressing an angry student body.

b) The manager of a fast food franchise whose business is failing.

c) The parent of a deaf-mute child.

2 Try turning your gripes into plans for action. Make notes of the next five "discontents" you find yourself mentioning. Then at a later time try to find twenty different ways for resolving each one of them. (Brainstorming techniques will simplify this task...once you have found five ways, the remaining fifteen will be found almost automatically.)

3 Suppose that while out of town for a relaxing but budgeted weekend your car containing all your travel money, credit cards, luggage, etc., is stolen. Find at least ten ways to turn this apparent disaster into a positive or enjoyable experience.

Games for developing Wholeness

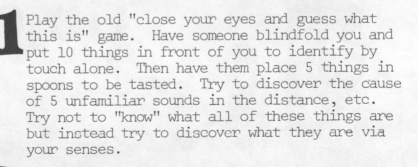

1 Play the old "close your eyes and guess what this is" game. Have someone blindfold you and put 10 things in front of you to identify by touch alone. Then have them place 5 things in spoons to be tasted. Try to discover the cause of 5 unfamiliar sounds in the distance, etc. Try not to "know" what all of these things are but instead try to discover what they are via your senses.

2 Try writing your name by placing a pen between your toes. You should immediately become aware of how children learn through their sense of touch.

3 Using multi-sensory images try to vividly describe the experience of eating an ear of buttered corn-on-the-cob or a rack of country-style spareribs.

4 Without speaking or writing, attempt to describe the essence of your belief regarding religion or the supernatural.

If you are predominantly right- or left-handed,
try thinking of that favored hand as being
representative of all that you already know...
the objective dominant, standing for all that
has been experienced, absorbed, named and
classified or interrelated. Allow your "other"
hand to be the sensitive subjective probe which
continues to examine the environment for clues
to physical characteristics. While "feeling"
with your subordinant "sensitive" hand inside
a paper bag filled with unknown assorted items,
use your dominant "knowing" hand to record your
discoveries. Attempt to become conscious of the
texture, temperature, form, size, weight of the
objects inside. Even try to identify the color
by touch alone. All the while remain conscious
of the separate roles of each hand. Then reverse
the roles and repeat the process. Do the items
now "feel" somewhat different? What problems
do your "other" hands encounter as they attempt
to feel or to write?

Guide to Measurable

Goals are usually stated in more or less unachiev-
able terms; i.e., a goal statement is a declaration
of an intentional result or outcome...it doesn't
tell you how to get there but merely where you
want to end up...tomorrow, next month, five years
from now, decades later on. Goals are reached
in stages; piece by piece, bit by bit. Each
step can be thought of as an objective along
the way. Therefore, if you know the stages
(objectives) and can measure their achievement...
one by one...you will eventually arrive at your
goal.

Objectives

To make objectives measurable it is necessary to make them specific and clear. Simply, you can think of objectives as the work determined as important or necessary to reach the goal. For example, a college may define a curriculum of courses (objectives) required to obtain a degree (goal). Then each course will in turn define its separate objectives necessary for passing that course. Unless mutual standards are accepted, the task of translating goal statements into lists of clear and specific objectives is a personal matter...each person's requirements would differ from all others and standards for achievement would derive from common values, experiences and expectations.

The creative problem-solving (design) process can easily be viewed as a series of activities (objectives) leading to a goal (redefined intentions). Beginning with the tasks of acceptance and analysis and ending with the tasks of option generation and selection, implementation and evaluation.

As an exercise, try listing the objectives you might have to reach if you intended to reach one of the following long and short range goals:

> cooking a special meal for six friends
> buying a new bicycle
> learning to speak a foreign language
> designing a vacation house

As you can see, there are no directions in each of those typical statements...they must be translated into activities or the step-by-step process of getting there. To get the "special" meal or the "right" bicycle or learn to speak "well" or design a "truly good" house, it's going to be necessary to further define the quantity and the quality required of each objective along the way because only in that way will you be able to measure the accomplishment of your goal in a relevant way. For instance, the first objective involved in the "special meal" goal might be"to determine the likes and dislikes of the six friends...what they can and cannot eat, which of them are on a diet, etc." When you have such a list, that objective can be said to be met. Then on to the next objective, etc., etc.

Objectives outline the paths to your goals. For a more conscious trip, clear and measurable objectives are a necessity. But clear foresight is not always possible. That's where anxiety sets in. To lessen its impact, simply stop to review where you intend to ultimately end up, what tasks you have already accomplished and try to assess that amount of work which seems to still remain.

Some lessons learned from Problem-Solving...

by first-hand experience

1. Don't believe everything you hear.

2. Without having been there before, you may have to feel your way slowly.

3. Having been there before can stop you from finding new ways to get there.

4. You can relate the solution of one problem to other kinds of problems.

5. Just as the logical conscious thinking process can work for you, so can the subconscious or "chance" thinking processes.

6. You must learn to find a definition through analysis and not be misled by the initial statement of a problem.

7. You can define things by determining to see rather than to merely look.

8. When you relate your definitions of things to one another, you may find connections between them.

9. It can be helpful to have a rampant imagination; to turn things upside down; take them out of their context for a different look at them.

10. The subconscious imagination can be helped by the logic of the conscious mind just as it also works the other way around.

11. There are generally more ways than one to get to a solution.

12. A complete solution requires a combination of many diverse experiences.

13. If it doesn't work, try it again. You may have missed something.

14. Get all the facts. Try to be sure the problem is stated "truthfully."

15. Don't rationalize the success of a part to mean success of the whole.

16. Learning by doing is often faster (but not necessarily easier) than learning vicariously through others.

17. One thing leads to another.

18. Unpleasant memories can get in the way of discovering new experiences.

19. Intuition is the subconscious accumulation of past experiences.

20. All experience is permanently locked in the brain. Some of it is just "hard to get to."

by logic

1. The subconscious random sample of thoughts can be stimulating to a logical ordering.

2. It makes sense to set limits on your subconscious mind in order to get on with an intentional process (as long as the limits do not rule out "hot" ideas).

3. Logic alone does not insure creativity. Creativity is the purview of the "whole" mind.

4. Searching for an idea which can work for lots of things is often easier than searching for a solution to only one thing.

5. When you examine only part of a problem, it helps to have the whole problem in mind.

6. Proper assessment of <u>all</u> ideas is essential.

7. Losing your guide (security and habit) is one way to discover new paths.

8. A problem solution is dependent on the relationship of many subdecisions.

9. There is at least some form of relationship between all things.

10. Through the solution to one problem, we may find the solution to another.

11. It is easier to reach a goal when the path is clear.

12. Weak understanding can lead to false conclusions.

13. All things must be judged in terms of the "big picture."

14. The subconscious is always there to help when logic bogs down.

15. Solving the components is one way to solve the entire system.

16. To determine the solution to a mystery, you must find the essential clues.

17. Some attempts must be repeated many times before producing acceptable results.

18. Finding simple ways to deal with things can be helpful in complex situations.

19. Some problems are so connected to other problems that they cannot be considered by themselves.

20. A well-kept journal of a process provides an automatic product.

by planning

1. General principles can come in several or many different forms.

2. Experiment can produce the unexpected.

3. We can allow inappropriate principles to stand in the way of our search.

4. Although sometimes useful, subjective influences cannot entirely replace logic.

5. Although desirably balanced in an overall sense, a predominance of either subjective or objective influences will none-the-less exist.

6. Complex problems can often be defined as simply as apparently simple problems.

7. An assessment of the determining points of view is a proven way to a successfully complete solution.

8. You may need a computing machine to help solve some problems which exceed the capacity of your awareness. Some things just can't be dealt with properly without making many simultaneious comparisons.

9. Evaluation can eliminate much leg-work.

10. Experience often leads to quick but incorrect conclusions about new situations.

11. Experimentation can get things going when bogged down.

12. You can learn by doing. A proven method is to get started.

13. Advance assessment can stop a pitfall.

14. Thinking is dependent on a good balance of logic and experience: conscious thought and subconscious feeling.

15. The application of principles can greatly reduce the time for acquiring problem-solving experience.

16. Unproven principles can get us into trouble.

17. A good strategy is to expect the unexpected.

18. What you don't know but need to know is critical to successful solutions. Dealing with your ignorance in a conscious way should lead you to a keener awareness.

19. What appears to be is not always what really is.

20. Records help to prolong appreciation of experience. Always travel with some means of recording what you do.

SYNECTICS...

Synectics Education Systems
121 Brattle Street
Cambridge, Mass.   02138

One of the many separate problem-solving processes synthesized into the "universal" process presented in this book is SYNECTICS, a series of techniques utilizing analogy, metaphor and simile to develop solutions, alternatives and unique or fresh viewpoints. Derived by William J. J. Gordon, the Synectics process is an "excursion" through a sequence of three stages.

    In Stage 1 -- You examine initial viewpoints
                    You analyze the situation
                    You criticize and unload pre-
                      conceptions and
                    You restate your initial viewpoint

    In Stage 2 -- You "stretch" your limits by examining other problem situations without concern for your own situation...you get away from the situation that is troubling you

    In Stage 3 -- You return to your problem situation with the fresh experiences of other situations and apply that new energy to your own situation with the intended result of a new viewpoint

In short, Synectics is a process of developing "insight" by utilizing the technique of "outsight." The key to this process is the word "stretch"; a psychological attitude that it is easier to work on problems other than your own and that you can profit by applying solutions derived outside of your situation to solve your own situation.

According to Gordon, four paths to creative behavior are:

1. Detachment and Involvement
    Getting both outside the problem as well as inside the problem

2. Deferment
    Having consideration and tolerance for all manner of input

To uncover imaginative definitions for problems, find the problems within the problems. A problem is always made up of lots of little problems. For one reason or another, each of us will decide that one of those particular subproblems is more important than any of the others; thereby taking that one as our personal definition.

3. Speculation
    Having fantasies, posing questions, making
    suppositions

4. Cbject Autonomy
    Allowing the product being sought to
    become the process being experienced

The three "mechanisms" used to facilitate such
behavior are:

1. DIRECT ANALOGY
    Finding how one thing is related to another...
    discovering the ultimate interrelationship
    between all things

2. PERSONAL ANALOGY
    Becoming personally sympathetic to various
    situational conditions. Role-playing,often
    to the point of empathy to discover internal
    problems difficult to see from an outside
    view only

3. COMPRESSED CONFLICT
    Dealing with key sub-problems as an effort
    to resolve a total issue by way of solving
    its internal conflicts

SYNECTICS is a process wherein "the joining together
of apparently different and irrelevant objects"
is used as a means to formulating new views to
problematic situations.

If you are searching for a fresh point-of-view,
try the Synectics techniques of asking how your
situation is similar to very different things...
remembering to "stretch" as far as you can. A
problem in human relations might find unique
relationships in the corners of agriculture or
mechanical engineering. Asking how a financial
problem is like a plate of spaghetti is more
likely to reveal a fresh viewpoint than if you
tried to keep your attention glued to monetary
matters.

Try "getting into" the situation by allowing
yourself to "feel" the uniqueness of people,
things and situations outside yourself. The
strange experience of attempting to role-play
an object often reveals a hitherto unnoticed
sub-problem or relationship. Step outside your
situation in order to be able to view it as part
of a universal context and not merely as the
tough, isolated thing you may incorrectly imagine
it to be.

Procedure for Self-Hypnosis

Hypnosis in all its many forms is a universal
way for reaching the subconscious mind with
messages; it is the key to all mind-trips.
Whatever you are into or want to get into,
hypnosis can work as a basic method. Essentially,
it involves a process of convincing yourself of
your goals by freeing yourself of distraction
and fears and by getting to your conscious
behaving self through your subconscious self.
It is a relaxation technique and a learning-
discovery technique; the ultimate self-motivator.

Deep prayer, meditation, EEG feedback,
mind control, reevaluation counseling, Zen,
karate, yoga, positive thinking, ESP, cosmic
consciousness, etc., all begin with hypnosis
in one form or another. It's all a matter of
getting yourself into a "receptive state."
Then, when you are ready to receive, you tell
yourself what to do and begin to change accord-
ingly. Hypnosis can't make you go against your
own will. Rather it is a way for helping you
to hear what your will is saying:a "hypnotic"
state; somewhere between being awake (conscious)
and asleep (unconscious); the state of half-
asleep and half-awake or subconsciousness.
When achieved you are relaxed enough to allow
yourself to heed your own suggestion; where the
inner mind can concentrate on messages you put
there. What you are told to do in that state
is more impressive to you than when distracted
by the possible reality of negative consequences.

The basic procedure for self-hypnosis is as follows: (approximate time: 20 minutes)

1. State (perhaps in writing) your purpose; your objective for using hypnosis.
2. Get into the hypnotic state
   a) Relax--loosen clothing--lie down or stretch out and get as loose as possible
   b) Close your eyes (to block out external consciousness)
   c) Let go. Put your body to sleep. Tighten each part of your body from eyes and jaws to feet and then let them totally relax from the top of your head to your toes. Silence and darkness can help shut your eyes and other senses to outside stimulus.
   d) When relaxed, don't stop. Go deeper and deeper into your subconscious mind. Imagine your body to be "silly putty." Imagine that you are swaying gently back and forth in a hammock in a quiet garden or that you are slowly going down an elevator or stair which gets you deeper into sleep with each level. Allow your body to be numb; without weight, free of stress.
3. Then, plant your suggestions. Talk to yourself in a soft but firm tone. If this is too difficult, you may need a friend or a tape recorder to slowly and rhythmically tell you what you want to learn to do.
   If, for instance, your intent is to effect a change in behavior, mentally describe the desired behavior in detail. Make it vivid and visual.
   Imagine yourself going through the new behavior five times in succession. Step outside of yourself and watch yourself doing it one more time. Suggest some positive, rewarding experience as a benefit from the new behavior.
4. When your message has been inserted, wake yourself with confidence.
   a) Tell yourself that as you awake and get up, you will feel better, have greater confidence and that in general you are on a positive trip.

Since auto-suggestions only have a life-span of about 36 hours, until you truly learn to change your behavior you may need to reinforce yourself by repeating this process many times.

Try opening some new doors.
"Originality is simply a fresh pair of eyes." - Woodrow Wilson

117

How to Criticize Painlessly

The need for assertive criticism often emerges in the realm of conscious problem-solving.

Here is a fool-proof method for telling yourself or someone else that something is wrong without fear of losing a friendship or of starting a battle.

The trick is to place the criticism within a context of positive reinforcements...just simple diplomacy.

1. BEGIN WITH TWO POSITIVE REINFORCEMENTS
    "You really are a well-seasoned traveler."
    "You have all of the best gear for hiking."
2. INSERT YOUR CRITICISM
    "I wish we could stay in step when we hiked."
3. ADD ONE MORE POSITIVE REINFORCEMENT
    "I notice that you can adapt easily to most things."
4. FINISH WITH A RAY OF HOPE
    "If we work on this together, I'm sure we'll be able to get harmony into our stride."

A Communication Checklist

Creative problem solvers are often faced with the additional problem of communicating what they uncover to others. If you recognize this to be the case, and if you have wondered what to do about it, here's a guide that could help you along.

118

COMMUNICATION involves translating a meaning which is in your mind into a medium and through the environment to the mind of an intended receiver. The meaning is affected by your background and is formed by your ability as well as by the background and ability differences of the receiver.

IMPORTANT DETERMINANTS OF SUCCESSFUL COMMUNICATION SEEM TO BE:

- YOU, THE SENDER (knowledge and attitudes)

- YOUR ABILITY TO SHAPE AND SEND MESSAGES OF YOUR MEANINGS (skill)

- THE QUALITY OF THE MESSAGE (substance and relevance)

- THE SELECTED MEDIUM

- THE ENVIRONMENT (external elements which facilitate or block the message)

- THE RECEIVER'S ABILITY TO RECEIVE

- THE RECEIVER'S BACKGROUND AND ATTITUDES

SENDER AND RECEIVER BACKGROUND

Age, personal relationship to each other, expectation based on experiences
Attitude and potential ramifications or consequences
Beneficial outcome; motives, values, needs
Recent experience; uplifts, traumas, sickness, diversions, fatigue, anxiety, etc.
Habits, customs, rituals, taboos, prejudices, biases, assumptions
Education, travel experience, breadth of outlook
Influential aspects; idols, models, aspirations
Areas where influence can be affected
National, religious, racial heritage
Social attitudes, politics
Insecurities and strengths
Specific knowledge of message area
Concurrent focus of attention

SENDER AND RECEIVER ABILITIES (Skills)

Experience, breadth or scope of practice
Preferences related to training
Physical handicaps
Mental blocks
Vocabulary
Awareness; ability to relate to other interests
Propensity to distraction (attention span)

119

QUALITY OF THE MESSAGE
Content; completeness
Relevance to receiver familiarity
Facilitates recognition
    clarity
    simplicity
    strength of stimulus
    orderly

CHARACTERISTICS OF THE MEDIUM
Potential for sensory stimulation
Appropriateness to message content
Appropriateness to sender's skills, knowledge
    and attitudes
Within receiver's limits of acceptance
Energy required
Symbolic characteristics
Speed
Noise (distraction) characteristics

THE ENVIRONMENT
Harmony with message and sender-receiver
    relationship
Noise (distractions)
    movement
    sound interference
    temperature discomfort
    threat to physical or mental security
Pressure to perform

Need PEP ??
try...
...consulting a professional trip consultant.

maybe you need help with diet planning or physical fitness
> see a nutritionist, physical therapist or physician
> (books by Adelle Davis have helped others)

maybe you have a hang-up or mental barrier
> try a psychologist or psychiatrist; visit a counselling
> center; call a trusted religious leader or simply dial
> your local HOTLINE number

maybe you need other specialized help
> the local police? city administrators? consumer
> protection agency? organization? librarian?
> credit union?

Wiring Diagrams

Attempting to find direction, pattern and order is a constant task. All of us carry some "rules of thumb" along with us on our day-to-day problem journeys, using them as basic frames of reference to help us cope with new experiences or for categorizing and retranslating familiar experiences. They help us get a better hold onto reality by organizing its many bits and pieces into a manageable form.

A commonly used and familiar example is the knowledge that the sun rises in the east and sets in the west. When the sun is visible such knowledge becomes valuable as a replacement for a compass. It acts as a clock; it allows us to regulate physical comfort, becomes a guide for planning, etc. "Wiring Diagrams" are universal relationship finders; they simplify analysis. R. Buckminster Fuller reminds us that the only true specialist is the generalist; so start filling your personal bag of generalized principles as soon as possible. Fuller suggests beginning with a good engineering handbook. We suggest that you start by recording those you already use.

Some "wiring diagrams" we have found useful are given on the next pages.

A BASIC ABSTRACTION FOR THE CREATIVE PROBLEM-SOLVING PROCESS

Analysis	Concept	Synthesis
Take it apart	Decide what it means	Put it back together

1. ATTRACTION — become attracted
2. UNDERSTANDING — develop a meaning
3. MANIPULATION — apply your discovery

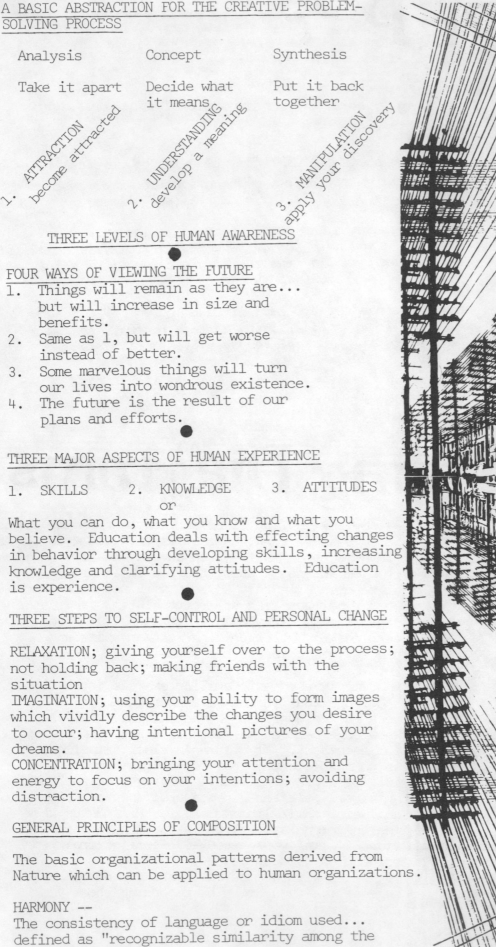

THREE LEVELS OF HUMAN AWARENESS

●

FOUR WAYS OF VIEWING THE FUTURE
1. Things will remain as they are... but will increase in size and benefits.
2. Same as 1, but will get worse instead of better.
3. Some marvelous things will turn our lives into wondrous existence.
4. The future is the result of our plans and efforts.

●

THREE MAJOR ASPECTS OF HUMAN EXPERIENCE

1. SKILLS   2. KNOWLEDGE   3. ATTITUDES
                  or

What you can do, what you know and what you believe. Education deals with effecting changes in behavior through developing skills, increasing knowledge and clarifying attitudes. Education is experience.

●

THREE STEPS TO SELF-CONTROL AND PERSONAL CHANGE

RELAXATION; giving yourself over to the process; not holding back; making friends with the situation
IMAGINATION; using your ability to form images which vividly describe the changes you desire to occur; having intentional pictures of your dreams.
CONCENTRATION; bringing your attention and energy to focus on your intentions; avoiding distraction.

●

GENERAL PRINCIPLES OF COMPOSITION

The basic organizational patterns derived from Nature which can be applied to human organizations.

HARMONY --
The consistency of language or idiom used... defined as "recognizable similarity among the parts of a whole"

CONTRAST --
The stimulation, conflicting and nutritive components...defined as "recognizable difference among the parts of a whole"

BALANCE --
The stability of interrelationships...defined as "recognizable equilibrium"

ORDER --
The systematic operation of the whole...defined as "recognizable pattern of organization"

UNITY --
The undeniable totality of the whole...defined as "recognizable wholeness" or "oneness"

●

THE GESTALT RULES OF VISUAL ORGANIZATION

Clear visual perception requires:

SIMILARITY --
Something alike about the parts of the whole

PROXIMITY --
Close togetherness rather than wide apartness of the components of the thing being organized

CLOSED FORMS --
All parts seen as complete and not partial; singular parts becoming wholes

GOOD CONTOURS --
Enclosures and lines must not be so complex or amorphous as to be difficult to reform in the mind

COMMON MOVEMENTS --
All parts should operate within the same organizational patterns

RELEVANT EXPERIENCE --
We tend to see only that which we are programmed to see

●

THE BASIC DREAMS AND EXPECTATIONS OF MODERN SOCIETY

1. TO BE ENGAGED IN CREATIVE WORK--something which may be looked upon as constructive

2. TO HAVE IMAGINATIVE LIFE-STYLE and be considered by others as being unique

3. TO HAVE A COMPLETE LOVE AND SEX LIFE--a total experience of intimate human relations

                        and

4. TO BE IN CONTROL OF SELF rather than the one controlled by others

123

Wiring Ahead

Use these pages to begin your personal collection
of "wiring diagrams." Begin with recording
those which you believe have potential for
simplifying the journey to your special goals.

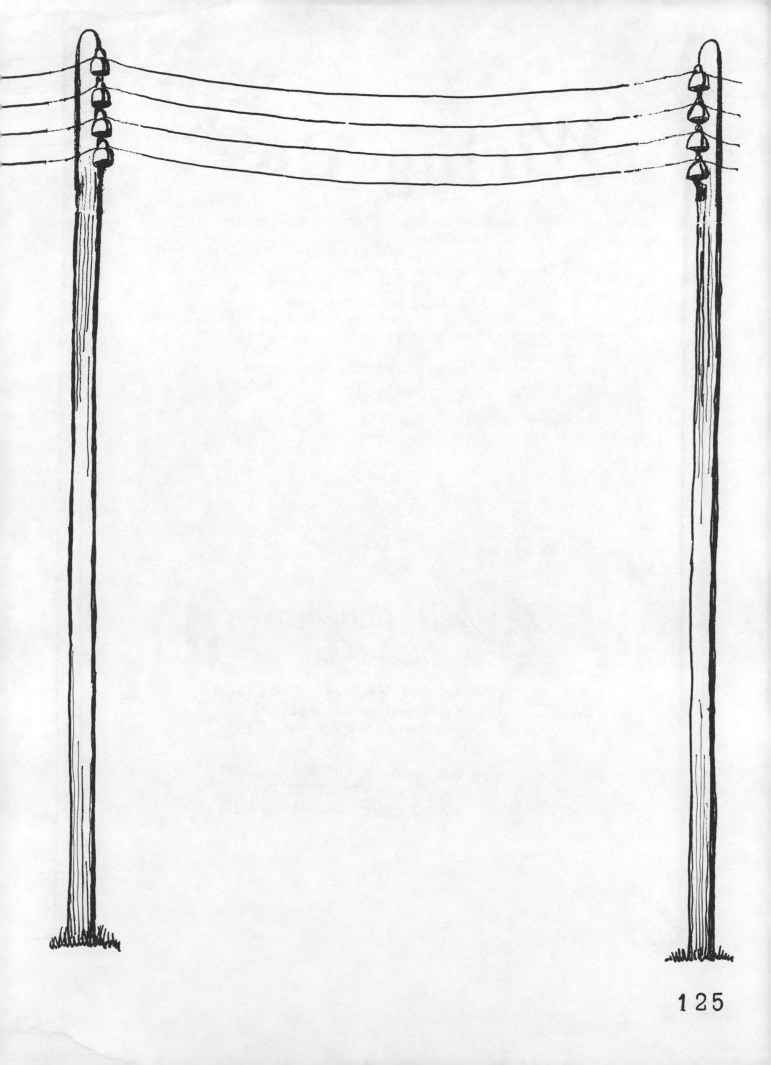

125

Wiring Back

If you have been learning to be more creative while reading these pages, you should be very anxious to do something "constructive" about one or more of your "discontents" with the material you have discovered in THE UNIVERSAL TRAVELER. We'd like to hear your thoughts. Write them down and mail them to us. (By writing your discontent you will also give yourself the opportunity to check whether or not your words are as good--or as bad--as your feelings.) We'll respond to all feedback.

Send feedback to...
Don or Jim

SCHOOL OF ARCHITECTURE and
ENVIRONMENTAL DESIGN
SAN LUIS OBISPO, CA. 93407
·or·
C/o WILLIAM KAUFMANN, INC.
ONE FIRST STREET
LOS ALTOS, CA. 94022

Acceptance. 17,20,36
Ad Valorem. 38
Alexander, C. 27,58,88
Alternatives. 67,77
Ambidextrous. 108
Analogy. 38,42,71,85
. . . . 111,114
Analysis. 17,20,46
Anxiety. 91
Aquinas, Thomas. 11
Archetypical Form. . . . 82,88
Art. 86
Attributes. 51,63,71,
. . . . 72,85
Autonomy of Object. 114
Awareness. 58,112
Balance. 86,102,123
Bionics. 82,87
Brainstorming. 68,73
Brainwashing. 82
Branching. 21
Checklist. 30,31,38,
. . . . 45,52,118
Circular Order. 20
Closed Forms. 123
Coffee. 32
Common Denominator. 88
Common Movements. 123
Communication. 95,118
Composition. 122
Compressed Conflict. . 114,115
Concentration . . . 40,115,122
Conformity. 40
Constructive Discontent . . 10,
. . . . 12,106,107
Contours. 123
Contrast. 86,122
Control. 123
Creative Behavior. . . 8,15,58
Creativity. 7,8,10,13,
. . . . 34,104
Criticism. 118
Curriculum 109
Cybernetics. 1

Declaration. 38,43
Defer Judgment. 68,114
Definition 17,19,20,
. . . . 21,59,92
Design Methods. 7,22,29
. . . . 30,38,48,62,
. . . . 68,76,82,96
Design Process. 8,16,17
. . . . 20,21,22,26,
. . . . 34,59,94,109,122
Detachment. 114
Diagrams. 86
Diary. 32,112
Do-It-Yourself Computer . . 85
Dreams. 123
Ego-Strength. 11
Energy States. 4,5,16,
. . . . 30,35,46,59
. . . . 66,74,80,94,101
Environment. 119,120
Essence 62,65,90
Essential Unit. 88
Evaluation. 17,18,20,
. . . . 21,76,78,94
Excellence. 109
Expectations of Man 123
Experience 31,33,110,
. . . . 122,123
Expert Consultants. . . .55,90
False Pride. 10
Fame and Fortune 44
Fear. 7,14,48
Feedback. 21,126
Forced Relationship. . . 49,72
Free-Wheel. 68
Freedom. 10,11
Fuller, R. B. 121
Games. 104
Gestalt. 123
Goals 1,17,74,
. . . . 102,109
Gordon, W.J.J. 28,58,
. . . . 69,114
Grades. 98
Grids. 88
Habit. 10,13,44,
. . . . 45,104
Harmony. 86,122
Holistic. 89
Human Needs. 89
Hypnosis. 40,46,
. . . . 116,117
Idea-Selection. 17,19,
. . . . 20,21,74
Ideas. 17,19,20,21,
. . . . 32,56,66,92
Imagination. 56,122,124
Implementation. . . . 17,19,20,
. . . . 21,80,115
Incubation. 92

Innovation. 114
Insight. 115
Inspiration. 92
Intuition 13,31
Key-Word 64
Keys 10,14,
      108,115
Language Guides . . . 4,5,26,30,
      37,47,60,67,
      75,81,95
Learning 50,102,
      114,116
Limits 111
Linear Order 20
Logic 15,111
MacKinnon, D.W. 10,28
Mager, R. 28,58,
      99,110
Magic 92
Manipulative Verbs 69
Matrix. 39,54,
      62,77
Measurable Objectives . . . 108
Medium/Message 119
Metaphor 114
Model 39,52,53,87,
      91,119
Morphology 53,72,85
Nature 122
Notation 91,92
Objectives 32,36,55,
      63,66,94,108
Objectivity 8,52
Order 20,86,123
Osborn, A. 28,68,
      73,92
Outsight 115
Pack Rat 49
Pattern Language 87,88
Patterns 54,122
Peanut Butter 32
Performance Specification . . 82,
      83
Personal Opinion 76
P.E.R.T. 78,79
Planning 112
Potpourri 77
Prayer 40
Prejudice 52
Pride 10,43
      48,105
Principles of Design . . . 86,
      123,124
Priorities 39,124
Problem 34
Process Oriented 23,40,
      102
Product Oriented 23,102
Progress 96,98
Proximity 123

Quality 96,98,
      104,120
Quantity 68,96,104
Question 48,51,62
Questionnaire 97
Receiver 119
Relaxation 116,122
Responsibility 11,39,41
Role-Playing 91,115
Rules-of-Thumb 121,124
Science 86
Scoring 77
Seale, Bobby 10
Self-Belief 10,11,104
Self-Discipline 10,11
Self-Hypnotism 40,45,116
Self-Image 119
Sender 119
Sensitivity 56
Seven Deadly Sins 11
Similarity 123
Simile 114
Sleep 32,116
Soft-Systems 1
Speculation 114
Spiral Continuum 21,94
Squeeze and Stretch . . . 57,62
Stanislavsky, C. 38,44
Stretch 115
Structural Limits . . . 90,91
Sub-Problems 64,87,115
Subjectivity 8,52
Sun 50,121
Synectics 28,49,69,
      91,114,115
Synthesis 122
Tag-On 68
Tape Recorder 117
Time-Task 25,82,83
Topsy 82,91
Tourist Traps 31
Travel Guides . . . 4,5,27,30,
      45,58,79,93,99
Travel Tips 4,23,30
Trial and Error 92
Truth 111
Unit Growth 89
Unity 86,123
Universal Method 30
User 65,76,78
Wholeness 8,9,10,
      12,107
Wiring Diagrams . . 122,123,124
Why 57,62
Yoga 117
Zwicky, F. 28,73